Alastair Frew is a partner in Lodders' Real Estate group. He heads up the Business Property Team and specialises in advising commercial developers, business owners, niche housebuilders, and private investors together with the banks and institutions that fund them. Alastair created and leads the Renewable Energy team at Lodders, guiding landowners through the complex documentation required to create a solar PV development, battery storage scheme, wind farm, or the installation of gas generators or anaerobic digestion equipment on their land.

A Practical Guide to the Law on using Commercial Property for Electric Car Charging and Solar and Wind Power

Second Edition

A Practical Guide to the Law on using Commercial Property for Electric Car Charging and Solar and Wind Power

Second Edition

Alastair Frew

Solicitor

Law Brief Publishing

Published 2024 by Law Brief Publishing, an imprint of Law Brief Publishing Ltd
30 The Parks
Minehead
Somerset
TA24 8BT

www.lawbriefpublishing.com

Paperback: 978-1-916698-37-6

PREFACE

In this revised second edition, I have taken the opportunity to add more information and material regarding the generation of electricity from large scale solar farms.

Landowners continue to be approached on a regular basis with promises of untold riches if the join the new green energy revolution. If they hand their land over to a specialist developer, then before long they will start receiving a healthy income, as clean, green electricity is generated, or clean, green electric cars are silently re-charged on their land.

If only it were that simple.

In this book, I will take you through the processes for installing electric car charging points and for generating renewable electricity. I will point out some of the areas of concern and give guidance about current market practices.

All those electric cars need charging, and demand for EV charging points remains high. All that electricity needs to be generated, and solar panels, wind turbines and huge storage batteries are needed up and down the country.

All of this provides opportunities for landowners looking for a new income stream. It also provides a challenge for conveyancers, who are now being faced with a series of new legal documents. Many of these documents look similar to the ones we have seen dozens of times before, but with strange new clauses and confusing terminology.

The purpose of this book is to explain this new marketplace, and to provide practical hints and tips to conveyancers acting for landowners.

The law described is correct as at 31st May 2024.

I have been interested in green energy for as long as I can remember. It is nice to be able to go to work each morning knowing that I will be doing my little bit to help the planet as we try to move to a low carbon economy.

Alastair Frew
June 2024

CONTENTS

INTRODUCTION

Renewable energy schemes are really just landlord and tenant development projects, with a twist. The twist relates to electricity. The land deal is a means to an end. The purpose is the creation and transfer of electricity.

When advising clients regarding electricity schemes, whether power generation or electric car charging stations, it is worth remembering a little bit of secondary school physics: the number of watts generated is equal to amps multiplied by volts.

In other words:

Watt = Amp x Volt

The power generated is the total of the amount of electricity passing through the wire multiplied by the potential energy of the system.

That's it!

CHAPTER ONE

WHAT IS "RENEWABLE ENERGY"?

The best definition of 'renewable energy' can be taken from Directive 2009/28/EC of the European Parliament and of the Council of 23 April 2009. While the UK is no longer a part of the EU, this definition has been carried over into UK law.

Renewable energy is energy from renewable non-fossil sources, namely wind, solar, aerothermal, geothermal, hydrothermal and ocean energy, hydropower, biomass, landfill gas, sewage treatment plant gas and biogases, each of which are then defined separately within the Renewable Energy Directive.

Nuclear power is not fossil based and is not therefore excluded from the scope of "renewable energy". The point is rather moot and can quickly become absurd – while nuclear energy does not use fossil fuel and is almost carbon-neutral, it is not "renewable", while geothermal power is deemed to be renewable even though it actually is not – it may be almost limitless in its supply but is not actually "renewable."

To complicate matters further, Refuse Derived Fuel (post-consumer rubbish) or agricultural biomass is certainly renewable and non-fossil, but generating electricity by burning it releases large quantities of carbon into the atmosphere. RDF is only "green" in the loosest of senses. The industry will point to carbon-capture technology and the recycling of carbon by the process of growing new feed-crops, but these arguments do not convince everyone.

The UK is one of the big hitters in global terms when it comes to generating electricity from renewable sources. At the time of writing, Great Britain produces 40% of its electricity from zero carbon sources, being principally from wind energy. Solar power hovers around 5-10% during daylight hours, while burning or digesting biomass (including RDF) is typically around 8%. The 40% figure also includes a contribution from hydro-electric schemes, which were once thought to represent the future, but now contribute just 3% of our electricity. The nation's fleet of new nuclear plants seems to be progressing at a snail's pace, so as the last of our coal fired power stations is shut down, the shortfall will have to be made up by wind and solar.

As with many countries, we import large quantities of gas, much of which is burned to produce electricity, and we also import large quantities of electricity from France's nuclear facilities via a cable under the English Channel. Our renewable energy sector therefore has significant room for growth.

CHAPTER TWO

ELECTRIC CARS

Electric cars (or electric vehicles/EVs) are very much a technology of today. The UK is the world's 4th largest market for EVs by market share, and 7th largest by total numbers. Manufacturers such as Volvo and Jaguar have announced that they would only manufacture EVs, although the date of Implementation has slipped a little towards 2030. The throaty roar from a straight-six E-Type has been replaced by the whoosh of an iPace. The classic Volvo estate car will now be all-electric.

Climate change, whatever your view on the subject, is now central to HM Government's energy policy. In 2017, transport was the largest carbon-emitting sector of the UK economy, accounting for 28% of UK greenhouse gas emissions. Improvements in diesel engine technology had led to a steady reduction in this figure, but the penchant amongst consumers for ever larger cars has resulted in the emissions figure rising again.

EVs are seen as the answer. Despite being 4th in the global league table, in 2019 around 58.5% of licensed cars were petrol, 39.1% diesel and 0.8% were either hybrid or fully electric. At the end of January 2024, the figure for EVs had shot up to 15% of newly registered cars. Globally, EVs account for just under 10% with the market dominated by China's BYD followed closely by the USA's Tesla.

The assumption made by National Grid ESO, the company which operates our national electricity grid, is that the UK stock of EVs will be well in excess of 3m by 2030, with more than 37 million by 2050. The UK Government has stated that new petrol and diesel cars will be banned from sale in 2035, the original date of 2030 having been pushed back due to pressure from the car industry.

In this book, I am considering plug-in electric vehicles to be EVs. Self-charging hybrids are therefore not included in this definition.

If you are looking to charge an electric car, you can do so outside your home. You simply plug it into a standard domestic 3 pin plug, using the charging cable that will be supplied with the car. Like all appliances, electric cars have dedicated charging cables. In this case, the cable is called an EVSE (electric vehicle service equipment) cable, and it should be standard equipment with all electric cars.

Better than this, would be to have a wall-mounted home charging point installed at your home. Why? A dedicated home charging point provides a higher amp rating, so will charge the car battery more quickly, and more safely.

The EVSE cable is intended to protect the car battery from over-charging. The EVSE cable is more properly called an 'in-line charger' or 'portable charger', although people have a habit of calling it a 'granny cable'. The cable will be 5 or 10 meters long, with a domestic 3-pin plug on one end, and a EVSE plug on the other end. You plug one end into your house, and the other end to your car. The power will come through at 13 amps (depending, of course, on your domestic electricity supply) and your car will be slowly recharged. The EVSE will cut the power when the battery is fully charged, although that will take a long time using a 13-amp domestic supply.

The EVSE in-line charge cable should be kept in the boot of the car, so that you can trickle charge your car in almost any location. The problem is that they charge the car very slowly. Typically, an in-line EVSE charge cable will supply 10 amps of current (it must be less than 13 amps, or it will trip your fuse box at home). Put another way, 10 amps multiplied by a domestic rated 230 volts, gives a power output of 2.3 kw per hour. A small EV battery holds 30 kw/h of power, so it will take 12 to 13 hours for a full charge. If you top up your battery overnight every evening, this should be enough. Equally, if your EV is actually a plug-in hybrid, then this will be perfectly sufficient. It is however entirely inadequate if you drive a pure EV and need a quick turnaround after a long journey.

For faster charging, you could look to a dedicated charge point fitted at your home or office.

Whereas an EVSE cable plugged into a socket in your house would take 13hrs to charge your EV battery, it would take just 6 hours using a dedicated charge point to charge a 30kw battery.

Home charging points operate at 230 volts, being the voltage that is available in your house. So, it follows that the power increase is down to an increase in the current, from 13 amps to 16 amps. Remembering that Watts = Amps x Volts, if you are able to install a 32-amp charging point, then the charge time drops again, to three or four hours.

All of this refers to domestic 230-volt "single phase" AC electricity. For really fast charging, you need to use DC power.

Years ago, when Mr Nikola Tesla invented AC electricity, he did so in order to make electricity easier to transport. AC current alternates back and forth, so the total power load on the equipment at any given time is effectively zero. For charging electric batteries, this is of limited use. Good old fashioned Direct Current is the best thing for charging a battery. The irony; Mr Tesla invented AC, but you need DC to charge the huge battery within the EV named in his honour – the Tesla car!

DC electricity is difficult to transmit over long distances, and much more dangerous than AC if "mishandled." For this reason, the

National Grid transmits electricity using AC, just as Mr Tesla intended. When you plug your mobile phone into the 3-pin plug at home, the charging plug converts the power from AC to DC, so that your phone battery will charge more quickly. More powerful devices, such as tablet computers, will have larger plugs, so that they can provide more current (more amps) to charge the larger battery more quickly.

The problem is that the speed of charging while using an AC power supply is often limited by the ability of the equipment within the EV's On Board Charger (OBC) to convert AC to DC, and so to charge the battery. Some small cars have very advanced OBC equipment, allowing their small batteries to be fully charged at home in just a few hours. Conversely, some larger vehicles have a much lower conversion rate (and much larger batteries) meaning that the up-market driver might be off the road for a substantially longer period of more than ten hours for a full charge.

Annoyingly, while all EVs in Europe and the USA use the same standards for the equipment, the marketplace has not yet agreed on a standard plug socket; the dedicated charge point attached to the wall of your office, or indeed your friend's house, may have the wrong type of socket, requiring you to resort to your slow granny cable. China uses a different standard altogether.

It's just like trying to charge your mobile phone, laptop and tablet – they each need a separate cable, you need to buy everything from the same brand and replace them all every couple of years.

All of this is pretty unimpressive – owners of luxury electric cars will want to be able to charge their vehicles much more quickly.

Domestic power supplies are modest. Home electricity consumption is typically not very large so the electricity company only provides a small amount of power. Added to this, most households are busily consuming most of their available electricity all of the time anyway, running lights, computers, fridges, cookers and heating systems. There just isn't a great deal left for charging an EV. High speed charging at home remains a distant dream.

As well as the AC-DC issue, there is something called three-phase electricity. Our homes typically use a single-phase power supply, which allow for a maximum EV charging rate of 7kW, which is why many car makers limit their OBC inverters to 7kW, regardless of the size of the battery. Industrial buildings need much more power than this, and demand what electricians call three-phase electricity, which passes through three conductors on its way to the building from the National Grid. This allows for much greater levels of power, as is required by industrial users. Larger office buildings will also have three-phase power, which can provide up to 22kW of power. Three-phase electricity in the UK is 400 volts, enabling must faster charging than 230v domestic power. However, charging your EV outside a commercial building in the UK will always be a little slower than many of the advertised timings, which use data from the USA where they have 480-volt electricity.

The answer is the DC Fast Charger. Using electrical current that has already been converted to DC before it reaches the connection to the vehicle, the EV battery is able to accept the electricity much more quickly. Charging times may be 10 or 15 times faster using DC, as the electricity does not need to be converted within the car's On Board Charger.

Therefore, public charge points, and those found at office buildings, will always be capable of converting the AC current supplied by the National Grid into DC before sending it down the cable to the car. These conversion units (known as "Inverters") are very expensive, costing thousands of pounds.

Super-fast charging does of course damage the car's battery. To counter this, many famous brands of EV will advertise a battery capacity which is much larger than is actually available; as the battery degrades, new battery space is opened up, thereby prolonging its total life. The maximum capacity is however always something of an illusion, a piece of marketing hype. The holy grail of EV battery cells is to find a method of charging which does not cause the internal parts of the battery to corrode during charging. Scientists keep declaring to have found a solution, but the marketplace is yet to see a convincing product.

CHAPTER THREE

EV CHARGING POINTS

If you want to install a fast EV charger, you need to go back to the beginning of our story – do you have the three-phase power that you need to run an EV fast charger? As we discuss later, the upgrading of your local National Grid connection could cost you anything from a few thousand pounds to an eye watering £500,000 or more.

Installing a bank of EV fast charging stations is therefore not just a case of laying a concrete plinth and bolting on a few boxes that look a bit like petrol pumps. The electrical requirements of the development need to be carefully investigated. The feasibility, timescale and cost may not be your problem as conveyancers, but unless your client is ahead of the problem, the scheme will not be a success.

Commercial landlords are seeing significant interest from their tenants for the installation of EV fast charging points. Now that the UK Government has committed to end the sale of new conventional petrol and diesel cars by 2035, and with strong take up of EVs – 16% of all new cars sold In the UK in 2024 were EVs, with a further 7% if you include plug-in hybrids – it is quite a selling point for a commercial scheme to include EV fast charging points.

An EV charging station with ten chargers could foreseeably be visited by two hundred cars each day, all being charged from one grid connection. For those of you who like maths, if a fast charger delivers 125 kW of power for 8 hours each day, that means it is delivering 1000 kWh. From a medium voltage network of the sort typically found in commercial districts, a developer can easily operate 10 individual fast chargers, thereby delivering 10,000 kWh per day. That's enough for 200 "pretty good 100-mile top-up charges".

Whole service industries are growing up around the network of fast charging stations, just as happened with petrol filling stations in the past. One of the assumptions (as yet, still something of a pipe dream) is that EVs will be self-driving and also that they will be owned collectively. You won't own your own EV, you will borrow/hire a pool car. This assumption is behind the growing industry for EV cleaning and servicing, based on the assumption that car hire is about to become hugely more popular; a car hire depot in a dingy industrial location just won't do anymore. Whether or not collective ownership takes off, EV owners behave differently to owners of petrol or diesel cars – their sat navs are constantly looking for the next charge point, and journeys are planned accordingly. Coffee stops are dictated by battery life.

Dynamic pricing is another factor. Smart metering can direct you to re-charge your EV when the price tariff is low, which assists the National Grid to smooth out the demand curve and make best use of available electricity. A quick daytime top-up on the motorway can cost more than a full nighttime recharge at home.

Installation of EV Charging Points on Commercial Premises

Installation by the Tenant within its existing demise

Is your client a landlord of a single-let building? In such a case, the installation of EV charging stations is likely to require an application from the tenant for a licence to alter, which can be handled by the managing agent and conveyancer as with any other such application.

However, there are some important points to consider:

Licence to Alter or Licence to Install? – In many cases, the tenant Is seeking to install the charge point within the estate common parts, rather than within its own demise. If the lease is of a building with no external areas, then any charge point will need to be installed within the common parts. Therefore, the tenant's application will be for the grant of additional rights, rather than for consent to alter the demised premises. The landlord must consider whether or not the freeholder's covenants regarding the common parts will permit or prevent any such application. Indeed, some landlords will require that the tenant signs a lease of the footprint of the EV charge point, rather than granting a deed of rights to install and operate.

Rent Review – if the tenant has paid for the charging station and is required to remove it at the end of the term, presumably the improvement will be expressly disregarded at rent review. Is this how your clients want to treat it? It is worth considering the issue of obsolescence – is the landlord granting permission for kit to be installed that will be outdated and abandoned after just a few years? Might the landlord be better advised to contribute to the cost, and have some state of the art equipment installed? If the landlord does contribute, does this need to be reflected in the rent review clause?

Planning permission – as is the case with all tenant works, does the lease allow the tenant to apply for planning permission? Is planning permission even required? As we will discuss later, the short answer is that no planning permission is currently required for a standard wall mounted EV charging station on private property. However, a free-standing fast charger would require a planning application. What does your lease say about this?

Who is responsible for obtaining planning permission? In most cases this will be the tenant, but is the landlord to be involved in any way? Is the landlord simply covenanting not to obstruct process, or must the landlord become involved?

Repair – is the tenant to be responsible for repairing the charging station following installation? If the tenant has installed the kit, then the tenant is almost invariably responsible for its ongoing repair and maintenance. The tenant might argue that the new charging station is an asset to the landlord's wider estate and might seek a maintenance contribution from the landlord in return, or perhaps a reduction in service charge.

As we discuss in more detail shortly, it would be a breach of the permitted development rights within the planning regime to leave a disconnected EV charging point on your premises, whether attached to the side of your building or free-standing in the car park. In many cases, a commercial lease might require the tenant to "comply with planning legislation", but it would be a good idea to include a requirement for mid-term reinstatement of such equipment in a licence for alterations, so that the tenant is unable to walk away and disappear over the horizon leaving disconnected EV charging points which had been installed under PD rights, and therefore have to be reinstated upon becoming disused.

Insurance – does the tenant insure as part of its trade equipment, or does it get added to the landlord's buildings insurance with an increase to the insurance rent payable by the tenant? This is an issue which needs to be discussed with the landlord's insurer. In most cases, it will be the tenant's duty to insure, but it does depend on the drafting of the lease and exactly who owns the equipment.

Reinstatement and yield up – usually, the tenant will be required to remove the charging station at the end of the term and yield up a cleared site. However, depending on the length of the lease term, the landlord may wish to have the right to require that the kit remains in situ, as the manufacturers claim that the equipment will have a 25-year life span, so it will remain a valuable asset at the end of a ten-year lease term. The key question for the landlord is – who actually owns the kit? The charging stations may well be leased by the tenant from a third party. In any event, if the kit is part of the tenant's network, it would be of little practical use to the landlord. A hybrid position is more likely, with the tenant being obliged to remove all above-ground equipment, but to leave the fundamental infrastructure in place. The concrete plinth and below-ground cabling will be very useful to the landlord in the future.

Either way, the landlord should remember to document the exact nature of works being carried out, so that the exact location of all the equipment is known.

It is common for the landlord to require the tenant fully to reinstate, and then to rely upon a sensible negotiation as the lease nears expiry.

Having no reinstatement obligation is dangerous for the landlord. If the tenant knows that it can walk away without having to reinstate, then it might start letting standards slip in the final years of the term.

On this issue, as with so many others, your client needs the advice of a specialist surveyor, but it is your responsibility to raise the issue and to ensure that the point is taken.

Capital Allowances – if the charging stations belong to a rack-rent tenant, then capital allowances are typically not available to the landlord. However, if the reinstatement clause requires the tenant to leave it in situ, then the equipment can be treated by the landlord as a qualifying fixture in its capital allowances tax calculation.

Installation by the Landlord

Many readers of this book will be conveyancers acting for a commercial developer seeking extra green credentials, or for a landowner seeking to diversify income streams, rather than for an electricity company or distribution network operator. Equally, your client might be a promoter who is likely to sell on rather than develop out.

When investigating the legal title to the property, even though the EV charging kit broadly speaking just bolts onto a concrete plinth with very shallow foundations, you will still be required to undertake a full title investigation.

There will still be foundations penetrating into the ground, and the scheme will require underground cabling, so it is important to check to see if there are any rights to mines or minerals which might be affected. Specialist development lawyers are fully aware of the problems that can be caused by an innocuous entry in the Property Register of a Land Registry title which refers to the reservation of mines or minerals. Transactional lawyers may be less aware of the problem; those underground minerals (which can be numerous types of rock or soil, not just coal or ironstone) are owned by a third party. Even if it is highly unlikely that any licence for extraction would be granted by the local authority, the right to extract minerals can still be infringed by the foundations of a new structure. If that structure generates a lucrative income for the landowner, then the owner of the mineral rights might decide to bring a claim for trespass. It is therefore worth considering carefully and paying for an indemnity insurance policy if appropriate.

Electric car charging stations are part of the new green economy, but at the consumer end rather than generating power. They must be connected to the national electricity grid, where capacity is a vital issue. Is it your job to advise your client about this? Has someone else already given advice? If so, do you trust that third party's advice?

The landlord may wish to install EV charging points as a way of enhancing its estate, making it more desirable to potential tenants. A few years ago, the "must have" amenity was a communal lounge with WiFi, now it is becoming the EV charge points.

Installation by a Developer

In all but the smallest cases, the development of a bank of EV charging points is likely to be carried out by a specialist developer. In most cases, the EV developer will be looking to take a lease, rather than to purchase the freehold. The charging station will require a relatively small demise, which will no doubt become a keenly sought after in the market for the sale of freehold reversions, in the relatively near future.

The landlord receives a rent, while the operator funds all of the development costs. The developer takes the risks, while the landlord gains increased "footfall" from all of those visiting EV drivers, all of whom must be affluent given how expensive the EVs are at current forecourt prices.

The EV charging station is relatively small and, until such time as EV charger points become ubiquitous, their presence will give a certain "green-kudos" to the development, which landlords will no doubt be very keen to promote at all available opportunities.

However, while the operator will tell you how small and unobtrusive their site is, please remember that the operator will want a visible site on the highway frontage. This is valuable real estate, so landlords must sell it very carefully.

A good charging point operator will handle the complicated application to the electricity company for a connection to the Grid, known as the DNO (Distribution Network Operator) application. This saves the landlord a huge amount of hassle but does put give ownership of the DNO connection to the operator. If the scheme does not proceed, this can leave the landlord to be ransomed, as it does not have control of this vital piece of the puzzle. More on this subject later!

The operator will usually take on a full repairing obligation for the charging stations, as is the case with most tenants on commercial developments. Please note however that most operators in this sector are, almost by definition, new businesses. Your landlord client will need to take great care to satisfy itself as to the financial security of its proposed new tenant.

Pre-conditions – in almost every case, the transaction will be conditional on both the grant of planning permission and also the securing of any required grid connection. Does your client have planning permission? Does your client have a planning consultant, or is this your job to advise about? Is the deal conditional upon planning? Is it your job to know whether or not the site is likely to be given planning, or whether it is in a planning constraint area for reasons of protection of architecture or high-grade farmland? Will objections from neighbours prevent the grant of planning permission?

Planning permission – application for consent itself is a matter for a specialist, but the conveyancer needs to be aware of the likelihood of planning permission being granted, as this will have an impact upon contract negotiations. Equally, negotiation of rental/capital values is a matter for a professional valuer, but the conveyancer should keep an eye out for any values which appear to be out of the ordinary. Importantly, who should bear the financial risk in the event that the scheme is not able to proceed? In other words, who pays for all the reports, applications and surveys? In most cases, the developer or promoter will pay for everything, either then recouping the cost from the landowner upon completion, or by factoring these expenses into the offered rent.? Conversely, does your client want to self-fund the scheme in the hope that an operator will then pay a higher rent? If the scheme is funded by the developer, does the landlord expect to have ownership of all the planning documentation? Not all developers are prepared to cooperate with this.

As with all development projects, who has the final say as to whether or not the grant of planning permission triggers the completion of the lease? Does the developer have the right to "bank" the planning permission, or must the lease be entered into immediately following the grant of a consent? Does the developer have the right to decide whether or not the planning permission is adequate to trigger completion? Alternatively, does the landlord have the right to trigger completion unless the tenant can show that certain pre-determined milestones have not been hit. If planning is not granted, or is granted but subject to onerous conditions, is the tenant obliged to lodge an appeal?

Mortgagee consent – remember that the freeholder needs to obtain the consent of any mortgagee before granting the lease to the charging point operator. Importantly, mortgagee consent is also required for the granting of the required cable easements. EV charging station leases are still relatively unusual, so mortgage lenders may not yet have a standardised approach to the granting of such consents. Therefore, it would be a good idea for your client to make any application for consent sooner rather than later. Will the landlord's bank be required to co-operate with the developer/tenant's bank over who has the right to step-in, if the developer fails to proceed according to an agreed timetable? In the case of a small stand-alone scheme in the corner of an established commercial development, this is unlikely, but if the EV charging station is a key selling-point of a new development project, then the bank may take a stricter position. As we will discuss shortly, the landlord's bank may be expected to consent to enter into a "direct agreement" with the tenant's own funder.

If the landlord's bank gets bogged down in the details, it might actually make sense for your landlord client to seek to raise finance by charging another parcel in order to have the proposed EV charging station free from mortgage, so as to simplify the banking paperwork.

If the landlord owns a multi-let estate, then there are some wider issues to consider.

Service Charge – who pays for the works? If the works are being carried out by a developer, then the answer to this is obvious. However, if the landlord is self-developing, then is he or she able to recover the cost of the EV charging kit from the tenants, along with the costs of installation, on the basis that this is an enhancement to the estate? Perhaps, the landlord must install at his own cost, but can then recover the cost of ongoing repair and maintenance from the tenants? Does this right to recover stretch to professional fees?

Crucial in all of this is the issue of "who pays for the electricity?" The EV cable itself should be controlled by a chip and pin system, or a radio-frequency smart card (RFID), so that estate tenants can use the facility for an agreed price. Usage could be granted for free, if the landlord were able to charge the installation works to the service charge. If the EV chargers are able to be used by the wider public, with payment taken by way of a mobile phone App, then the tenants on the estate should not be expected to pay for the installation works. Indeed, they might argue for a reduction in service charge due to the increased usage of the estate road!

While we are discussing the issue of who pays, please note the terms of HM Revenue and Customs Brief 7 (2021) which was published on 25th May 2021. The electricity supplied for the charging of EVs in public places, such as filling stations or kerbside charge points, attracts VAT at the standard rate of 20%. An EV charged at home will use electricity with VAT charged at the lower rate of 5%. In either case, an employer cannot recover the VAT on this, as the supply is made to the employee and not to the business. The electricity used to charge an EV at an employer's office building will also attract VAT but the employer can recover the VAT which relates to the employee's business mileage.

Almost as important as the question "who pays" is the question "has the landlord remembered to reserve sufficient rights to allow him to close part of the communal parking area in order to construct the EV charging station? During the works period, the level of disruption might be considerable. Probably, most tenants will be co-operative (depending on the service charge implications) but there needs to be a balance between the parties' conflicting interests. Will the tenants permanently have to lose car parking spaces in order to free up the area occupied by the charging station?

Is your electricity supply good enough?

UK Power Networks advise that you need an electricity supply of more than 70kVA (that's 70kW of DC power, before it is converted to AC) if you want to install electric vehicle chargers in a staff car park. By way of context, that is the same as for the installation of customer freezers into a high street shop. Super-fast EV chargers for a commercial charging station will require a stronger supply.

Direct Agreements

Who is your tenant? Whenever preparing to sign a commercial lease for a development plot, the developer will typically offer to enter into an agreement for lease in the name of the main company. How many times have we seen this, only for a subsidiary to be substituted at the very last minute? Expect nothing different from a developer of an EV charging station. As EV technology is relatively new, even the "household name" operators are also relatively new companies. Keep an eye out as always for the substitution of a newly formed SPV, and ensure that you check the structure of the tenant's group of companies – is the SPV actually a "group" company at all? Be alert for this and advise your landlord client as to the risk that the SPV could be wound up and dissolved, leaving the site half built. Perhaps the developer can be persuaded to offer a parent company guarantee? It goes without saying that a guarantee is only as strong as the company which is giving it, and frequently a "parent" company will have no available cash at all, which makes enforcement of a guarantee extremely difficult.

In a large development, the developer tenant might be persuaded to give a security bond, provided by a bank or insurance company. However, be alert to the fact that such bonds are easily offered, but then seem to be the last piece of the jigsaw to be settled, leaving the conveyancer with very little time to give thorough consideration to the wording of the document.

Increasingly, as well as granting the lease, the landlord will be required by the tenant to enter into a further document with the tenant's funder. The purpose of this additional document is to enable the funder to step into the lease as if it had been the original tenant. This document is known as a "direct agreement". We are used to seeing such documents in complicated development agreements, and particularly in the construction collateral warranties which support them, but they are much less common in simpler landlord and tenant agreements. The tenant will explain that it can only proceed with the scheme if it obtains institutional funding, and that the funder insists that the landlord agrees to sign a direct agreement.

The landlord may well have devoted much time and energy investigating the covenant strength of its proposed tenant, only to find that it is now required to accept an as yet unspecified funding institution as its tenant for the remainder of the lease term. To make matters worse, the funder will commonly insist on the right to require a novation of the lease to its nominee!

Direct agreements are becoming increasingly common. Landlords should anticipate seeing a requirement for such a document in all of the leases described in this book. As for the drafting the lease might contain the following:

> *"Direct Agreement": an agreement between the Landlord, the Tenant and any Funder taking a charge or mortgage over the Property in such form as that Funder requires and which gives the Funder a right to step into or be assigned the Lease, in such form approved by the Landlord (approval not to be unreasonably withheld or delayed and having due regard to the Funder's requirements).*
>
> *"The Landlord will co-operate in good faith with the Tenant and use all reasonable endeavours to satisfy the reasonable requirements of any Funder in respect of such financing or refinancing without any additional payment being made by the Tenant (except payment of the Landlord's reasonable costs)."*
>
> *"The Landlord shall use all reasonable endeavours without undue delay to agree the wording of and enter into a Direct Agreement with any such Funder, the Tenant and any other relevant party in respect of this Lease."*

The direct agreement itself might be a little unnerving to a landlord and tenant solicitor, as it is likely to have been drafted by the banking department of a City law firm and may be almost as long and complicated as the lease itself. The principle is simple enough – the tenant's funder requires the landlord to accept the funder's nominee as the new tenant. The direct agreement typically gives the funder the right to step into the lease, and then to step back out again. At that stage, the funder can require the landlord to accept a novation of the lease rather than an assignment. As with a standard assignment, either all parties sign a single deed, or the funder's nominee sends a certificate to the landlord giving notice of the transfer and requesting that the landlord countersigns by way of acceptance. If you are acting for the landlord, please take care to ensure that the tenant does not have the right to vary the lease when any assignment or novation takes place – the direct agreement should give the tenant the right to pass the lease to its funder, but not to re-write the document.

Boiling down a twenty-page document to just a few lines, the fundamental clauses of the direct agreement might follow the following form:

> *Assignment*
>
> *Pursuant to the terms of its debenture, the Tenant gives notice to the Landlord that it has assigned its rights under this lease to the Funder ("Assignment"). Notwithstanding the Assignment, the Tenant will remain liable under the Lease to perform all the obligations assumed by it under the Lease until such time as the Funder notifies the Landlord that the security created under its debenture has become enforceable, it will, subject to the provisions of this deed, remain entitled to exercise all of its rights, powers and discretions under the Lease.*
>
> *The Landlord acknowledges receipt of the notice of the Assignment and confirms that it has not received notice of any other assignment and consents to the making of the Assignment.*
>
> *Suspension*
>
> *The Landlord undertakes that it shall not take any enforcement action without first delivering written notice of intention to take*

such action ("Termination Notice") to the Funder specifying the grounds for such enforcement action.

Following the delivery of a Termination Notice, the Landlord undertakes that it shall not take any enforcement action during the period of 40 days following the date of such Termination Notice (the "Required Period").

If, during the Required Period, the Funder delivers a Proposed Novation Notice to the Landlord, then the Required Period will be extended until the Replacement Tenant becomes a party to the Lease.

During the Required Period, the Landlord undertakes to comply with all of its obligations under the Lease in accordance with its terms.

Step-in and Step-out

The Funder may deliver a Step-in Notice to the Landlord during the Required Period. On the expiry of 5 business days after the date of such notice, the Funder shall become a party to the Lease with all of the rights of the Tenant under that agreement. The Funder shall be jointly and severally liable with the Tenant for all of its obligations under the Lease. The Funder shall on the expiry of 5 business days after the Landlord has received written notice from the Funder be released from any obligations to the Landlord arising under or in connection with the Lease and this deed and the rights of the Funder as tenant shall cease, subject to any arrears or liabilities existing at that date.

Novation

At any time during the Required Period the Funder may give notice of novation ("Novation Notice") to the Landlord.

After it has served a Novation Notice, the Funder shall, to the extent it is available to the Funder, supply such further information relating to the Replacement Tenant as the Landlord may reasonably request.

If the Landlord does not approve a proposed Replacement Tenant, the Landlord shall notify the Funder in writing within 5 business days after the delivery of the Novation Notice setting out the reasons for its objection.

The Tenant and the Landlord shall each be released from further obligations to the other under the Lease and their respective rights against each other shall be cancelled.

The Landlord and the Replacement Tenant shall each assume obligations towards each other and acquire rights against each other in the same terms as the Lease.

The Landlord undertakes that it will perform its obligations under the Lease for the benefit of the Replacement Tenant instead of the Tenant.

The Replacement Tenant shall make payment in full of all arrears and shall assume performance of all the obligations and liabilities of the Tenant under the Lease.

The Landlord shall permit the charging of the Lease in favour of any bank or other funder providing finance to the Replacement Tenant.

For the avoidance of doubt, the Landlord agrees that such transfer shall not of itself give rise to any right to terminate the Lease.

New Direct Agreement

The Landlord and the Tenant or Replacement Tenant shall, at the request of the Funder, enter into an agreement on substantially the same terms as this deed following any refinancing or any novation of the Lease.

Transfer certificate

The Replacement Tenant accepts and procures the transfer to it of all of the rights, title and interest of and all of the obligations of the Tenant under the Lease.

The Replacement Tenant requests the Landlord to accept this transfer certificate as being delivered to the Landlord pursuant to, and for the purposes of the Direct Agreement so as to take effect in accordance with the terms of the Direct Agreement on the Effective Date.

The Replacement Tenant warrants that is has received a copy of the Lease, together with such other information as it has required in connection with this transaction and that it has not relied and will not rely on the Funder in relation to its entering into this transfer.

The Replacement Tenant undertakes to the Landlord that it will perform in accordance with the terms of the Lease all obligations of the Tenant under the Lease which it is assuming under the Direct Agreement.

Exclusivity Agreement or Option?

Exclusivity Agreement

The landlord may be asked by the EV charging point developer to grant an exclusivity agreement.

During the planning process, the developer can get on with its application, safe in the knowledge that the landlord cannot sell to anyone else. Having received a token premium, perhaps as little as £1.00, the landowner might think that it is in control because there is no obligation to grant the tenant a formal lease.

In fact, the tenant controls the planning application process and owns all of the associated documents. As the end of the short term exclusivity agreement approaches, the tenant/developer may well start to bargain for a reduced rent; it could easily walk away upon expiry.

Therefore, the landlord's solicitor should include provisions into the exclusivity agreement requiring the developer to proceed swiftly with its planning application and/or electricity grid connection application. Developers are very resistant to such clauses, which are also very difficult to enforce. Developers are very adept at spinning matters out to suit their own objectives.

The whole point of an exclusivity agreement is to prevent the landowner from negotiating with potential rivals. If the exclusivity period is too short, then the developer has little incentive to spend large sums of money. If the period is too long, then the developer can also use this in order to drive down the rent by delaying matters until the landlord concedes.

These are issues of fundamental importance. The landowner must strike the right deal with the right developer. As a conveyancer, it is your job to raise these points, although the final decision must be for your landowner client with advice from its surveyor.

Might an option agreement be better?

Yes, possibly, provided that the terms of the intended lease been agreed in advance and are annexed to the option, with an agreed rent figure, or at least an agreed rent mechanism. If not, and the problems referred to above still apply – the developer will have control of the planning and grid connection process, and has complete exclusivity, which it can use to drive down an open market value calculation.

How long should the option period be? Really, this is not something that a conveyancer should be giving advice about, although we are asked for our opinion almost every time a set of heads of terms are produced. Sometimes it appears that the parties pluck a figure out of the air. If the developer needs 12 months, then they will ask for three years on the basis that 12 months quickly becomes two years and it would therefore be nice to have three years. A very hard-nosed landowner might insist on 12 months and only 12 months, but this might result in the developer walking away. Just as likely, and even worse, the developer might agree to the landowner's strict terms but then invest very little time and energy in the scheme. A year later, nothing will have happened, and your landowner client's tough stance has only achieved a wasted year. Perhaps, the landowner should be more obliging, in the hope that the developer can be persuaded to try a little bit harder to secure a valuable planning consent.

Typically, the option will be for three to five years, although this period can often be extended to allow for a planning challenge to be heard. It is a hard-nosed landowner that refuses to allow for at least a 12-month extension in such circumstances.

Does the developer agree to pay an option fee? If so, is it enough? Again, it is not the job of the conveyancer to negotiate the level of the fee, but your client is almost certain to ask your opinion on the subject. If the developer is prepared to pay a large fee, and to have that sum released to the landowner, then this is highly compelling. However, if the option fee is to be held as stakeholder, then is the developer really venturing anything other than a little bit of negative cash-flow?

The landowner might prefer a small option fee which is then not deducted in the final calculation, to a larger option fee which manifestly will have to be paid for by way of a lower sale price or annual rent.

The landowner client's accountant should be consulted – perhaps a large sum now in return for a lower return later is a good bargain, producing vital income now, even at the expense of a lower total return. If the scheme is for a high value freehold scheme, which is perhaps a little unlikely unless the site is in a city centre location, the accountant should also be asked to consider whether the option payments should be staged across tax years, being mindful that a contractual obligation to pay an option sum triggers a tax liability as if the full sum were in the hands of the recipient, even if the payments themselves are staged over a period of months or years. The tax bill might in certain circumstances be higher than the first instalment. This is not necessarily a deterrent to the landowner, but it is an issue which must be fully understood.

Will the development need to run cables across third-party land? If so, whose job is it to secure the necessary cooperation of such landowners? The Electricity Act 1989 does provide electricity companies with compulsory purchase powers, if they need to acquire a wayleave or to purchase land. However, for all but the very largest schemes, the electricity company is highly unlikely to consider using its compulsory powers, so it will be up to the landowner and the developer to negotiate with the various neighbouring owners. The option agreement should specify whose duty it is to obtain these wayleaves.

Site access is also important. The existing access to the site may be sufficient for the existing user. If the site does not directly abut an adopted highway, do you need a new easement to permit the proposed new user? Even if the site does abut the highway, is the point of access physically adequate to enable all the additional vehicles to get in and out? As part of the planning process, a highway consultant should be involved, to ensure that the new vehicle movements are possible. The highway authority will of course be consulted by the planning authority as part of the planning process, so you must ensure that your client has taken specialist advice at the earliest opportunity, rather than just leaving matters until the planning application has been made.

Depending on the size of the scheme, you might need a separate access point for the heavy construction traffic, to allay the concerns of local residents about noise and dirt during the build-phase. Are you able to provide any assurances about this?

As a related issue, will the construction traffic cause problems to your other tenants? Will the tenants demand a service charge reduction, or assurances regarding the cost of repairing any damage to the estate roads? Please raise these issues with your client at the earliest opportunity.

If large equipment is to be brought to site, temporary access arrangements might be required, for the equipment or any necessary lifting gear. Again, has this been considered?

Works Compounds

How will the developer actually carry out the project? Aside from the perhaps more obvious issues of getting construction traffic into the site, another sting in the tail might be the need for a construction or works compound. Developers often overlook this, or deliberately fail to mention it.

Once everything is signed up, the developer may casually observe that the scheme can only be implemented if the landowner also supplies a certain acreage for construction equipment to be stored during the period of works, for no additional charge. Does the landowner have a works manager who can be involved at an early stage?

How large must this works compound be? For how long will it be required? If these issues are raised early, then a separate value can be negotiated.

If a works compound is created, the landowner should ensure that the developer is responsible for putting it back into good order at the end of the agreed period of use. Has anyone checked to see if the required parcel is actually vacant? Is it currently let on an informal basis to a commercial occupier? Perhaps it is let to an agricultural tenant, who will be very quick to insist on being paid proper compensation for loss of the acreage and for loss of any crops in the ground.

Depending on the ground conditions, the developer might need to remove large quantities of soil, in order to level the site or to remove any contaminated materials. Is your client able to assist by providing a nearby location for the dumping of non-contaminated spoil? If so, who is prepared to certify the quality of that spoil? Has your client obtained a licence to accept that spoil on its land? Remember, it is a criminal offence to dump materials in an unlicenced location, and that the offence is committed by the landowners as well as the haulage contractor. There are exemptions which permit the re-use of certain types of construction waste as hardcore in a redevelopment project, but if the rules are not adhered to, your clients will potentially be committing an offence even if the materials are not contaminated (known as "Qualifying Materials", as they can be lawfully dumped in return for the payment of a lower rate of landfill tax). If all that is being removed is clean, good quality soil, do the parties care who owns it as long as it is lawfully transported and disposed of? Such material has a market value but is also expensive to transport. Given the precise location of the development site, is the ownership of spoil important? Has your client thought about it and/or engaged a surveyor who can give more detailed advice?

If the EV charging station is being developed at the same time as the rest of the site, can the landlord provide any construction materials such as sand and gravel, which might be found elsewhere on the wider property? Again, it is not for a solicitor to give engineering advice, but these are issues which need to be raised.

VAT – it is very important that the landowner communicates to the developer its VAT status. Developers and tenants always prefer not to pay VAT where possible, even if they can reclaim it from HMRC at a later date. If the parties discuss the situation fully, it may be possible to agree a mutually beneficial VAT strategy. Perhaps, the landowner can revoke a long-standing but never utilised election? Remember of course that if the agreement with the developer contains a promotion agreement, then the fee claimed out of sale proceeds by a promoter will attract VAT, which is payable by the landowner.

The Lease itself

The demise – how big is the site? Typically, the site will just be a few square metres, but is there room for expansion, or just for the initial kit?

Term – the tenant will want a term of at least 25 years. This is because 25 years is roughly the anticipated life expectancy of the charging stations.

As for drafting, here are a few examples of the type of wording you might expect to see:

> *"Access Road" the access road to be constructed by the Tenant in accordance with clause 3.6.3 and a licence for alterations to be entered into between the Landlord and the Tenant and shown edged in purple on the Plan and referred to in Schedule 2;*
>
> *"Cables": all electrical plant and underground electric lines (as defined in section 64 of the Electricity Act 1989) installed or to be installed by the Tenant at its own cost along and to the Premises or Estate and all apparatus appurtenant to the Permitted Use;*
>
> *"Charging Station": each of the 10 rapid charging stations to be installed at the Premises;*
>
> *"Equipment": the Charging Stations together with any permitted additional or replacement equipment which the Tenant may from time to time install on the Premises;*

When it comes to the calculation of the estate service charge, even though the demise will be small but with a disproportionately high level of vehicular traffic, the tenant may be expected to pay a sum based on the area of the demise:

"Tenant's Proportion": the proportion the Premises measured in square feet bears to the aggregate of the gross internal area of all units on the Estate and the external area of the Premises, that are either let or, if unlet, are or were constructed or adapted for separate letting from time to time, measured in accordance with the Code of Measuring Practice issued by the Royal Institution of Chartered Surveyors and the Incorporated Society of Valuers and Auctioneers as amended from time to time;

Repair

The Tenant shall keep the Property in good and substantial condition and repair, and at all times clean and tidy and clear of all rubbish;

Access Road

At its sole costs to construct the Access Road and to no lesser specification than as set out in the documents annexed having first obtained all statutory authorisations within 12 months following the date of this lease subject to the obtaining of the Landlord's consent as to the route, specification and standard of construction.

Equipment

The Tenant may install, replace and operate the Equipment (including signs relating to the Equipment and the Premises) at the Premises without the consent of the Landlord but any other alteration or addition to the Premises shall require the consent of the Landlord (such consent not to be unreasonably withheld or delayed).

Parking restrictions

The Tenant must not permit any vehicles belonging to any persons calling on the Premises to stand on the Estate Roads so as to cause an obstruction.

Rights granted to the Tenant

As well as all the usual rights which a tenant on a commercial estate would expect, the EV charging station lease might have the following wording:

The non-exclusive right for the Tenant and all those authorised by it including its customers to pass and re-pass with or without vehicles, plant and equipment over the Access Road between the adopted highway and the Premises and to park a vehicle on the Premises for the purpose of gaining an electric charge.

The right to the supply of electricity to the Premises.

User

You may expect to see wording such as one or other of these alternatives:

"Permitted Use" the erection and operation of the Equipment for the charging of electrical vehicles and the parking of vehicles for the duration of such charging only.

"Permitted Use" the use of the Premises as a station for the provision of electricity or other power or fuel for the charging, fuelling or propulsion of road vehicles with ancillary vehicle valeting (including car vacuum machines, air / water towers and similar services).

Alienation

> *The Tenant must not assign or charge part only of the Premises and must not underlet either whole or part only of the Premises PROVIDED THAT the Tenant may underlet part of the Premises in the event a substation lease is required to be entered into with the distribution network operator on the distribution network operator's standard terms and for the purposes only of an electricity substation.*

Alterations

Does the lease allow the tenant to replace and upgrade the kit, or to increase the number of charging stations, or is the landlord imposing a very strict user clause? During the term of the lease, it may be impossible to predict the technological advances that will be made, but is the landlord prepared to allow the tenant to do whatever it wants with the site, provided that it remains an EV charging station? The operator-tenant will want the right to upgrade the kit without landlord's consent, perhaps conceding that there is to be a maximum number of individual stations.

What about having "double-sided" stations which can be used by 2 cars at once? Perhaps, the size of the demise will address this problem, as there may only be enough space for one car per station. This is reminiscent of the debates which we used to have regarding telecoms masts; remember that in the end, the law stepped in and prevented landlords from prescribing the nature and quantity of kit which could be installed. While nothing has been proposed by this current Government, I anticipate that a future Government will introduce legislation at some point in the medium future, to protect the rights of EV charging point operators, at the expense of their landlords.

The landlord will try to be as restrictive as sensibly possible, but please remember when drafting the agreement for lease/option that the parties may not be able to specify exactly where the stations will be installed. It would be wise to allow the tenant a degree of flexibility, as the exact location of the kit will ultimately be decided by the underground electricity supply cabling, which is controlled by the District Network Operator (DNO) rather than the parties to the lease. Once constructed, the landlord may then be able to exercise a greater degree of control regarding any future changes.

In return, for the tenant paying a generous rent for the EV charging station, the Landlord may agree to an exclusion zone where there will be no other charging points. Here is some possible wording:

> *During the period of three years from and including the date of this Lease, the Landlord may not allow any part or parts of the exclusion zone edged in green on the lease plan to be used for the provision of a further charging point or points for electric vehicles.*

Crucially, the tenant may require the landlord to co-operate with the laying of a new electricity supply. Here, a wayleave may be vital:

> *If requested to do so by the Tenant due to the requirements of an electricity distribution network provider and for the Permitted Use, the Landlord shall together with the Tenant enter into a wayleave with an electricity distribution network provider in such form as shall be approved by the Landlord and the Tenant shall indemnify the Landlord for any costs and future liability incurred in relation to the same.*

Rental values

Rent will typically be linked to the number of car charging stations installed. As with the "user and alterations" clauses, it is never possible to future proof a site, particularly when dealing with a new technology. Is the rent fixed (subject to standard review clauses) or is it instead linked to the total power drawn? Given that this may remain constant, as it depends on the DNO connection, it might make sense to charge a turnover-style rent based on the number of vehicles charged. As technology improves, and charge times fall, this could result in a significant increase in throughput. The tenant will object to this – asking why it should be charged extra rent if the enhancements to the kit have been paid for by the tenant itself. In a "standard lease", the tenant is not charged extra rent for any tenant improvements. With an EV charging point lease, the tenant will expect to be asked to pay "rent per car charged", or at least a "rent based on annual profit". This requires monitoring; the tenant will know exactly how many cars have been charged, and how many watts have been drawn, but will need to divulge this information.

Currently, the market norm seems to be for a fixed rent together with a top up based on annual profit. This may well evolve over time. As a point of reference, electricity generation leases commonly fix the rent by reference to the number of watts generated, using a series of bands, rather than an absolute sliding scale.

EV users will typically find the charging station by using a mobile phone app. Such apps can enable owners of private EV charging points to allow passing EV drivers to charge up, typically for a fee of £5. Landlords could make it a condition of granting licence for alterations to its tenant that any such income is shared with the landlord. Alternatively, the tenant might keep all this income, but pay a higher estate service charge due to increased wear on the estate road. The app will enable usage data to be provided to the owner of the EV charge point, so the landlord should require sight of such data.

As well as for the service charge figures, in order to calculate a profit rent, the landlord needs to have sight of all of the information. The EV car drivers will pay for their electricity by App or credit card and the tenant will want to deduct the App administration charges from its gross income figures. Equally, the kit itself may be leased, so there will be equipment rent and/or finance charges to bring into the equation.

Once the tenant has calculated its net profit, then an agreed percentage is to be paid to the landlord. In some leases, the tenant pays the higher of the basic rent and the profit rent, while other leases require the tenant to pay both basic rent and profit rent. Naturally, if both rents are to be paid, the profit rent will be paid at a lower percentage than in leases where the tenant only pays the higher of the two rents.

A further question for commercial landlords is this: does the lease prohibit such third party use, which is otherwise unconnected with the general use of the property? Is a service charge hike sufficient compensation for the landlord, or should the rent increase as well?

If the parking areas are outside the tenant's demise, standing within estate common parts, then the tenant would need to be granted an express right to install, with ongoing rights for access and maintenance. Should the tenant then be obliged to repair the equipment? How does this impact upon the landlord's right to re-allocate parking spaces in the future, given that the new charging stations are surely to be reserved only for that specific tenant?

As well as the obligations for repair and reinstatement, will the new charging point attract additional traffic, and therefore require an adjustment to the estate service charge? Does the lease allow the landlord to vary the insurance rent percentages, to reflect the potential increase in risk due to the presence of the charging station.

As with all alterations, have the parties considered the impact upon a future rent review? If the kit is paid for by the tenant, then presumably they should be rent neutral.

What might these clauses look like?

Rent

> *"Additional Rent" means the amount (if applicable) of the Rent Percentage of the Net Profit in each Profit Period that is greater than the Base Rent in each calendar year;*
>
> *"Base Rent" the annual rent of £25,000.00 (being equivalent to £2,500.00) for each of the 10 Charging Stations) as reviewed to the higher of open market values and the Base Rent as increased in accordance with increases in the consumer prices index] plus any Value Added Tax from time to time;*
>
> *"Base Rent Review Dates": each anniversary of the dates of this lease and "Base Rent Review Date" means the relevant Base Rent Review Date;*
>
> *"Net Profit" means the aggregate of all sums of money or other consideration received or receivable for the use of the Premises from the business of charging of electric vehicles at the Premises and from all business of any nature whatsoever conducted at, in, from or upon the Premises by the Tenant less direct costs relating to the Premises including the cost to the Tenant of leasing, maintaining and repairing the equipment, transaction processing fees payable to third parties and VAT;*
>
> *"Rent Percentage" means 10%.*

Regardless of the number of Charging Stations which are operational at any given time, the Tenant will pay the basic rent to the Landlord without deduction set-off or counterclaim on the usual quarter days by equal quarterly payments in advance.

The Tenant shall produce a Profit Certificate to the Landlord upon each anniversary of this lease failing which the Landlord may produce a reasonable estimate of the Net Profit.

The Tenant shall pay the Additional Rent being the Rent Percentage of the Net Profit within 14 days of each anniversary of this lease.

There are estate management issues to consider. Even if the EV charging station is located on prime frontage land, does it require 24-hour security? Depending on the location of the site, the planning permission may permit 24-hour operation. If so, will the presence of motorists driving onto the site enhance general site security, or will this become a magnet for car thieves? Will the equipment itself require to be protected from theft or vandalism? Your landlord client should consider this carefully in conjunction with its insurers, but also should bear in mind the views of the other tenants on site. Will an increase in security costs provide them with any tangible benefit, or must they accept this in return for an increased level of traffic into the development?

When the lease is finally signed, does the tenant have the right to terminate? Will the landlord grant the tenant a break right, in return for the payment of a rental penalty? Upon exercising a break, what does the lease say about yielding up in good repair? Some standard wording might be:

Yielding up – At the termination of the Term, the Tenant shall yield up the Premises with vacant possession cleaned and

> *repaired in accordance with the provisions of this Lease and if so requested by the Landlord with all apparatus and equipment either removed or rendered permanently safe and in accordance with the Tenant's obligations in this lease in respect of repair and maintenance.*

Many EV charging leases will also require the tenant to provide a bond to secure the cost of this remediation. We will discuss this in more detail in relation to solar farms.

As with all development projects, EV charging station developers want total flexibility for minimum payment, whereas landlords want the maximum payment for minimum flexibility. Exactly where the final balance is struck depends very much on the nature of the landlord's site, and what other users are already on site.

Security of tenure

If the tenant is purchasing kit and having it installed on the wall of the landlord's building, then this is not an issue, but if the tenant leases the equipment from a third party then the landlord could find out that the EV charging station has acquired security of tenure, even though the office building it serves has a tenancy which is outside the security of tenure provisions of the Landlord and Tenant Act 1954. This will come down to a question of fact – do the new charging points have their own demise?

Stand-alone EV charging stations will be businesses, so the leases will create tenancies which benefit from security of tenure under Part 2 of the Landlord and Tenant Act 1954, unless an exclusion agreement is entered into. Given that the lease is likely to be for a term of 25 years, is the landlord prepared to allow the tenancy to benefit from security of tenure?

The EV charging station operator may well want a contractual right to renew the lease, for a further 25-year term. This does not necessarily require the landlord to grant a lease which has security of tenure; the tenant might have a contractual right to renew, which may also give it the right to renegotiate the basis of the rent calculation. This is different from having a statutory right to apply to Court for a new lease for a term of up to fifteen years, and at current market rent. Given the likely changes in technology over the next twenty-five years, what will the market rent be in the future? Telecoms leases boomed in value, but rental figures have now dramatically softened, as technology permitted a huge increase in the "reach" of each site causing first a boom in values and then a slump as the market became saturated. Will the same happen with EV stations, when super-fast charging finally becomes a reality? What government regulations will be introduced in order to control market forces?

Ending the Lease or Relocating the Equipment

The landlord will want the right to terminate the lease, as with all business tenancies. However, the tenant has installed equipment which is disproportionately valuable given the rental values, so the tenant's funder will want protection. Very much like a "mortgagee protection clause", the landlord may be required to give notice to any such mortgagee or sign a direct agreement as we discussed earlier.

> *If the whole or any part of the Rent or any other sum payable by the Tenant under this lease is unpaid for twenty one days after becoming payable ... then (subject to any Direct Agreement) the Landlord may re-enter the Premises and thereupon the tenancy created by this lease will determine but without prejudice to any rights of the Landlord in respect of any antecedent breach of any of the Tenant's obligations in this lease provided that before re-entering the Premises pursuant to this clause, or commencing*

> *any proceedings for forfeiture of this lease, the Landlord shall give notice of the breach complained of to any mortgagee of this lease of whom the Landlord has received notice and if the mortgagee confirms in writing to the Landlord within 14 days of the notice that it wishes to remedy the breach, allow the mortgagee 28 days (or such longer time as may be reasonable in view of the nature of the breach) to remedy the breach.*

The landlord might want to redevelop its estate. Here, we may see a "Lift and shift" clause:

> *If at any time during the Term the Landlord wishes to redevelop the whole or any part of the Estate the Landlord may terminate this lease by giving to Tenant not less than three months' prior notice in writing and on the expiry of such notice this lease will immediately cease and terminate but without prejudice to any claim by a party in respect of any antecedent breach of any obligation of any other party under this lease provided that on or before the expiry of such notice the Landlord will grant to the Tenant a new lease of an alternative site no less commodious and accessible by motor vehicles than the Premises ("Alternative Premises") for a term of years equal to the period then unexpired of the Term but otherwise such new lease will be in the same form and contain the same provisions and covenants (mutatis mutandis) as those contained in this lease. The Tenant as soon as reasonably practicable thereafter complete the erection of the Equipment on the Alternative Premises subject to successful planning and satisfactory grid applications and remove the Equipment from the Premises or render the same safe.*

Please note that typically the Landlord will be required to pay the costs for the preparation of the new lease including any Stamp Duty Land Tax and Land Registry fees as well as the costs of the dismantling and decommissioning of the Equipment and the erection of a new

Equipment. Please note that if your client has any plans to relocate the electricity substation or associated cabled, even if the substation lease contains a lift and shift clause the costs of the relocation will be very significant.

Planning Permission and Building Regulations for electric vehicle charging points

Do you need planning permission to install an electrical charging outlet?

Schedule 2, Part 2, Class D of The Town and Country Planning (General Permitted Development) (England) Order 2015 (as amended) states that planning permission is not required for the installation of a wall mounted electrical outlet for recharging of electric vehicles as long as the area is lawfully used for off–street parking.

For installation to be classed as permitted development, the electrical outlet (and its casing) must not exceed 0.2 cubic metres or face onto and be within two metres of a highway.

Are the regulations the same for a free-standing electrical charging outlet? The regulations refer to these as "upstand mounted outlets".

Schedule 2, Part 2, Class E of The Town and Country Planning (General Permitted Development) (England) Order 2015 (as amended) states that planning permission is not required for the installation of an upstand with an electrical outlet mounted on it for recharging electric vehicles, as long as the area is lawfully used for off–street parking.

For installation to be classed as permitted development, there must be no more than one electrical upstand per parking space, and the equipment must not exceed 2.3 metres in height from the level of the surface used for the parking of vehicles. This limit is reduced to 1.6 metres where in the curtilage of a dwelling house or block of flats. As with a Class D installation, the equipment must not be within two metres of a highway.

As is typically the case with permitted development rights, neither Class D not Class E grant rights to properties which are listed or are within a site designated as a scheduled monument.

With this important caveat in mind, the result is that most offices with private parking areas, as well as most homes which have a driveway, can have an EV charge point installed without requiring the grant of planning permission.

Under both Class D and Class E, when the electrical outlet is no longer required as a charging point for electric vehicles, the wall (on which the outlet was mounted) or the land (on which the upstand was placed) must be returned to its previous condition (prior to the installation being carried out) as soon as possible.

A commercial tenant would therefore not need to apply for planning permission to install an EV charging point but would probably require a licence for alterations.

What about building regulations?

The New Homes (New Development Standards) Bill 2019-21 was brought before Parliament by Private Members Bill in June 2020 but has not yet been passed into law, having only received its first reading as of March 2021. The draft legislation picks up similar requirements from EU directives and expressly deals with residential development. However, the associated draft technical guidance for Building Regulations would require that for all new non-residential buildings (whether or not part of a mixed use scheme or a purely commercial scheme) with at least eleven parking spaces, must provide at least one electric vehicle charge point. In addition, there must be "enabling infrastructure" (or a complete charge point) for every five parking spaces. These charge points and the enabling infrastructure must comply with all other building regulations and electricity cabling standards.

In other words, any commercial property with parking for eleven cars will need electrical capacity for two charging points. One concern might be that these draft regulations simply encourage developers to provide no more than ten car parking spaces, with larger car parks having fourteen or nineteen (etc) spaces in order to avoid having to put in that additional charging point.

Very importantly, the draft building regulations will also apply to major renovations, if there are more than 11 parking spaces and the renovations affect the car park or the electrical installations to the car park or the associated building.

The charge points must have a capacity of at least 7kW. This seems like a bit of a "miss" by HM Government, as a 7kW charge point can be run off a standard domestic supply, so will not supply the fast charge that visitors to a modern commercial building will expect, which would require a 22kW charger at the very least.

New electrical standards for the earthing of charging points

The regulations regarding protective multiple earthing (PME – which refers to the use of multiple earthing points for a single neutral conductor cable) have been changed by way of an amendment to British Standard BS 7671:2018 – Section 722 (Electric Vehicle Charging Installations).

"Regulation 722.411.4.1 concerning the use of protective multiple earthing (PME) supply has been redrafted. In addition to changes to the existing information, two new indents have been added:

(iv) – to cover a single-phase installation, and

(v) – to allow the use of an alternative device to those in (iii) or (iv) which does not result in a lesser degree of safety than using (iii) or (iv)

Regulation 722.411.4.1 does not allow PME to be used to supply an EV charging point unless one of the methods described in (i), (ii), (iii), (iv) or (v) of 722.411.4.1 is used.

The new and amended requirements around PME are intended to keep pace with technology, while increasing the ability for an installer to use PME on EV charging equipment installations. This means that more charging points can be installed, helping the rollout of EV infrastructure across the country."

With better earthing, by virtue of increased use of PMEs, more voltage can safely be put through the cabling, allowing for an increased number of EV charging points to be installed at the new location.

The future for electric vehicle charging stations?

EVs are the future; hydrogen powered cars are not appealing to the public, and the combustion engine is being phased out.

Many people predict that the next big thing will be the wireless charger. We charge our mobile phones wirelessly, and wireless EV chargers are now on the market. Perhaps remarkably, they are no less efficient that Type 1 and Type 2 chargers, despite there being no physical connection. If such stations could be installed within/under city streets it would allow fast charging without having dangerous cables trailing across the footway. However, you have to park your car in exactly the right spot, which could be difficult in practice.

Wireless charging is ideally suited to buses, taxi ranks and commercial fleets with guaranteed parking spaces. Private car parks are anotherr likely location, where the technology is not so essential, but would be highly desirable.

The downside of having numerous charging stations buried under the tarmac, is that the industry has currently worked its cost/profit calculations on the premise that drivers will park up, plug in and then purchase an expensive coffee and cake while waiting. If you can charge up while waiting at the traffic lights, these assumptions will need to be changed. A landlord who makes a substantial investment in an EV charging facility might find that the cash generation fundamentals are totally changed if wireless charging starts to become commonplace.

Despite this potential to upset the commercial applecart, the Government has been providing fairly significant grant funding to enable feasibility studies into wireless charging projects. The outcome is that the technology is shown to work; what remains to be seen is whether it is adopted, and by whom. Anything installed on/under a highway will clearly have to be done with the co-operation of the highway authority, and also without interfering with all the other utility services already buried beneath the surface of our roads. It may therefore not be the answer to the question of how to get a mass-market availability of charging stations for those many EV owners who do not have a private driveway, but it might be a very useful solution for commercial fleet operators.

Substations

Does the tenant's innocent application for a licence to assign end up railroading the landlord into signing a wayleave for the supply of electricity, and the digging up of an estate road for the installation of the new cabling?

If new cables are to be laid, the electricity company will require an easement over your client's land, or indeed a neighbour's land. Some landowners refuse to grant an easement, preferring to sign a wayleave instead, on the basis that a wayleave is a simple contract that can be determined on notice, whereas an easement is a registrable disposition of land, and generally is granted in fee simple, and therefore permanent.

In many cases, the landlord will be presented with a contract which grants an easement for the same fixed term as that of the development site, with clauses permitting the landlord to require it to be removed at the end of this fixed term, with the land being fully remediated. Often, the remediation is only for equipment that is on the surface or within 1metre below the surface.

However, the documentation might also contain innocuous clauses which say that the tenant can call for a grant to the District Network Operator. The effect of this is that the easement would instead be granted to the statutory electricity company, and on the standard terms required by the DNO. The easement would now become permanent.

The DNO is also very likely to require a substation. This substation would be installed at the cost of the electricity company, in return for a 99-year lease, or (increasingly) freehold transfer. If the sub-station plot is being transferred as a freehold, then almost certainly the cable route would be granted by a permanent easement rather than a terminable wayleave.

Whether this matters or not very much depends on your client's attitude to granting such long-term contracts. It is not unheard of for landowners to withdraw from a transaction when it became apparent that their nice income generating scheme would in fact involve the construction of a substation that would be on site for a century or more.

If the site is a family-owned farm, and the substation is to be installed within the farmyard, or within sight of the farmhouse, then this point could easily scupper the whole deal.

If the site is purely a commercial development, then this is perhaps less of a problem – that said, I have experience of a commercial scheme that was delayed for many years because of the presence of a square of concrete laid in an out of the way location. It was laid by the DNO following the granting of a 99-year lease by the freeholder and was intended to house an electricity substation for a "Phase Two" which then did not happen. When the development scheme finally came back on track some years later, the substation was no longer required, and the "square" was needed for valuable development. The problem was that it had been let to the electricity company for 99 years, and the DNO had based its electricity planning for that district on the assumption that this substation could be installed and brought on stream at the required point in the future. It took my developer client years to persuade the DNO to surrender the lease, and this only happened after another nearby development had also granted the DNO the right to install an alternative substation.

As mentioned earlier, it is possible to negotiate a lift and shift clause. Here is a suitable clause, taken from an electricity substation lease:

- *The Landlord may from time to time during the Term give notice to the Tenant designating an alternative part of the Landlord's Property as the location of the Sub Station and/or an alternative route or routes for any of the Tenant's Service Media which must not be materially less convenient for the Tenant.*

- *Following receipt of a Relocation Notice, the Tenant must carry out and complete such Relocation Works in accordance with the terms of that Relocation Notice.*

- *The Landlord must pay the reasonable and proper costs and expenses incurred by the Tenant in connection with the carrying out of any Relocation Works on a full indemnity basis (including any irrecoverable VAT) within 10 working days of demand.*

As mentioned earlier, the engineering costs of carry out the relocation will be very significant.

Planning permission for substations

Does your client need to obtain planning permission for a new substation?

The DNO has certain statutory powers which give it permitted development rights for the installation of new substations or underground cables. The Town and Country Planning (General Permitted Development) Order 1995 (Class G Electricity undertakings).

For large substations however, the DNO must obtain planning permission from the local planning authority, while most overhead cabling schemes require planning permission from the Department for Energy & Climate Change. For high voltage overhead lines of 132kV which run for more than 2km, the planning application must be to the Major Infrastructure Planning Unit.

However, the DNO has PD rights to install substations of up to 29m3 in size and lay underground cables without the need for planning permission. The DNO can also connect individual businesses to the Grid by way of new 11kV overhead lines, under PD rights.

As you might anticipate, there are limitations to these PD rights in environmentally sensitive areas, or adjacent to rivers, canals, railway crossings and at environmental or archaeologically sensitive sites. Furthermore, the works must not adversely affect protected animals or habitats.

The text of The Town and Country Planning (General Permitted Development) Order 1995 is set out below:

> *Class G Electricity undertakings*
>
> *G. Permitted development*
>
> *Development by statutory undertakers for the generation, transmission or supply of electricity for the purposes of their undertaking consisting of—*
>
>> *(a) the installation or replacement in, on, over or under land of an electric line and the construction of shafts and tunnels and the installation or replacement of feeder or service pillars or transforming or switching stations or chambers reasonably necessary in connection with an electric line;*

(b) the installation or replacement of any telecommunications line which connects any part of an electric line to any electrical plant or building, and the installation or replacement of any support for any such line;

(c) the sinking of boreholes to ascertain the nature of the subsoil and the installation of any plant or machinery reasonably necessary in connection with such boreholes;

(d) the extension or alteration of buildings on operational land;

(e) the erection on operational land of the undertaking or a building solely for the protection of plant or machinery;

(f) any other development carried out in, on, over or under the operational land of the undertaking.

G.1 Development not permitted

Development is not permitted by Class G if—

(a) in the case of any Class G(a) development—

(i) it would consist of or include the installation or replacement of an electric line to which section 37(1) of the Electricity Act 1989(1) (consent required for overhead lines) applies; [note: being an electric line which has a nominal voltage not exceeding 20 kilovolts and is used or intended to be used for supplying a single consumer] or

(ii) it would consist of or include the installation or replacement at or above ground level or under a highway used by vehicular traffic, of a chamber for

housing apparatus and the chamber would exceed 29 cubic metres in capacity;

(b) in the case of any Class G(b) development—

(i) the development would take place in a National Park, an area of outstanding natural beauty, or a site of special scientific interest;

(ii) the height of any support would exceed 15 metres; or

(iii) the telecommunications line would exceed 1,000 metres in length;

(c) in the case of any Class G(d) development—

(i) the height of the original building would be exceeded;

(ii) the cubic content of the original building would be exceeded by more than 25% or, in the case of any building on article 1(5) land, by more than 10%, or

(iii) the floor space of the original building would be exceeded by more than 1,000 square metres or, in the case of any building on article 1(5) land, by more than 500 square metres;

(d) in the case of any Class G(e) development, the building would exceed 15 metres in height, or

(e) in the case of any Class G(f) development, it would consist of or include—

(i) the erection of a building, or the reconstruction or alteration of a building where its design or external appearance would be materially affected, or

(ii) the installation or erection by way of addition or replacement of any plant or machinery exceeding 15 metres in height or the height of any plant or machinery replaced, whichever is the greater.

G.2 Conditions

Development is permitted by Class G subject to the following conditions—

(a) in the case of any Class G(a) development consisting of or including the replacement of an existing electric line, compliance with any conditions contained in a planning permission relating to the height, design or position of the existing electric line which are capable of being applied to the replacement line;

(b) in the case of any Class G(a) development consisting of or including the installation of a temporary electric line providing a diversion for an existing electric line, on the ending of the diversion or at the end of a period of six months from the completion of the installation (whichever is the sooner) the temporary electric line shall be removed and the land on which any operations have been carried out to install that line shall be restored as soon as reasonably practicable to its condition before the installation took place;

(c) in the case of any Class G(c) development, on the completion of that development, or at the end of a period of six months from the beginning of that development (whichever is the sooner) any plant or machinery installed

shall be removed and the land shall be restored as soon as reasonably practicable to its condition before the development took place;

(d) in the case of any Class G(e) development, approval of details of the design and external appearance of the buildings shall be obtained, before development is begun, from—

(i) in Greater London or a metropolitan county, the local planning authority,

(ii) in a National Park, outside a metropolitan county, the county planning authority,

(iii) in any other case, the district planning authority.

The Grid Connection – Form G99

I have mentioned the term "grid connection" several times so far, but what exactly is it?

Put simply, a grid connection is a commercial contract with the DNO, allowing your client's site to be connected to the national grid. The largest schemes are connected to the Grid by way of a "transmission connection" which is negotiated directly with National Grid rather than the DNO, but for the majority of landowners, the G99 route will be relevant.

If you are lucky, there will already be a nearby substation with plenty of electricity capacity, and all you need to do is install a bit of cabling.

Very often however, the grid in the vicinity of the proposed scheme will not be able to support the anticipated increase in demand, whether for the use of electricity from the grid or the supply of power to the grid.

Contestable Works

One of the crucial elements of an application for a grid connexion is the specification for the engineering works themselves. It is not simply an application to ask the theoretical question "is their capacity" but will contain detailed engineering specifications. The engineering works can be divided into two categories known as contestable and non-contestable works.

Contestable works are those which can only be carried out by an accredited contractor (known as an accredited Independent Connections Provider or ICP) but they do not need to be carried out by the DNO itself. Contestable work will include:

- design for the network extension and any reinforcement works to the existing network if that is in itself contestable;
- procuring and supplying equipment and materials so we come on digging trenches and site preparation;
- installing substations;
- constructing the network extension and reinforcement to the network so we come on making records of all the work that is done and the location of all underground equipment;
- reinstating the site after the works had been carried out; providing locations and connexion points for metering equipment;
- attending to legal documentation.

Non-contestable works include items such as:

- the adoption of the new equipment as part of the public network;
- connecting the new equipment to the wider grid;
- network reinforcement, if this is not contestable;
- designing any works which are not fully contestable;
- reviewing and agreeing the legal documentation;
- monitoring testing and inspecting all contestable works.

The difference between these two categories is important. The electricity company will allow an ICP to carry out the contestable works, under its watchful eye, while the fundamental design must be to the specification of the electricity company. The decision whether or not to turn on (energise) the equipment is the decision of the DNO.

A full list of ICPs is maintained by Lloyd's Register, which operates the National Electricity Registration Scheme.

In terms of cost, there can be quite a stark difference. Depending on the scheme, the non-contestable works typically amount to about 10% of the total cost of the connection works. The applicant therefore has the ability to decide whether or not to leave the remaining 90% also in the hands of the electricity company, or to seek competitive tenders from the list of approved contractors. If the total bill is £1 million, that would mean that approximately £900,000 would be for the contestable works and therefore potentially open to competitive tender.

The grid connection is therefore both important and expensive. But who owns it?

Have your clients already signed away their rights to ownership of the grid connection to their property? If they have already signed a grid connection agreement, then you need to advise them carefully as to its terms – does the electricity consultant now own the grid connection? Does that consultant have the right to profit from the upcoming scheme? If the grid connection is still owned by your clients, do they have a specialist electricity consultant on board, in order to negotiate the suitable arrangement with the electricity network operator? It goes without saying that without a suitable electricity connection, the scheme cannot proceed.

The electricity grid connection right is granted to the applicant, rather than to the landowner. In many ways, this is similar to a planning permission. The trap that some landowners fall into is allowing their energy consultant to complete and submit the crucial form G99 (previously, the application form was G59) to the DNO. Once granted, the grid connection will then belong to the consultant rather than to the landowner, and this grid connection is personal, and non-assignable. Therefore, your landowner client should be made aware that, if it does not have control of the G99 application, then it could find itself ransomed by the third party energy consultant. All of this is fine if the consultant is paying the bills, but often the landowner will engage a consultant on the basis that all costs are the liability of the landowner, but that the consultant will send in the form G99. Without making any capital investment whatsoever, the consultant has successfully taken complete control of the development.

The upshot of all this is that, by allowing an energy consultant to make the G99 application, your landowner client may have unwittingly given away ownership of the vital electricity connection, and also obliged itself to entering into an easement across its land and the selling of a freehold plot for a substation. All of this, in order to secure a 15-year lease for a few electric car charging stations!

CHAPTER FOUR

WHERE WILL ALL THE ELECTRICITY COME FROM?

As the law currently stands, there will be no new cars sold with an internal combustion engine after 2040, so by 2050 there will be virtually no internal combustion engine cars on British roads. As EVs are far more efficient in their use of energy, this should result in a 75% reduction in total energy demand for road transport. EVs do use more energy in the production phase, due to the power required in the manufacture of the batteries. Even so, the latest research suggests that an EV is still 65% more energy efficient than a traditional car over its whole life cycle, if the energy cost of producing and transporting fuel oil are included and on the assumption that the vehicles are recycled – fuel oil, once burnt, cannot be reclaimed and recycled, while an electric battery can claw back a large amount of its huge initial manufacturing "energy footprint" by being recycled. Given that nearly two thirds of all mileage covered in the UK is by car, the increasing use of EVs will have a vast impact upon the nation's energy usage.

But, do we have enough electricity to enable us to replace all that petrol and diesel?

Load Factors and Low Inertia

A phrase which we will all be hearing more regularly is "Load Factor" – this is the amount of electricity generated as a proportion of the maximum potential generation. Good old-fashioned gas-fired power stations have a load factor of around 70%, while nuclear power stations get close to 75%. By contrast, the figure for solar PV is just 11%.

Meanwhile, wind power is a huge energy source for the UK. On shore wind farms have a load factor of around 20%, while off-shore wind farms achieve 40% with the very largest turbines showing a load factor of closer to 50%.

In response to the looming climate crisis, the UK Government has ordered that all gas-fired electricity generation should cease, but this leaves the country facing a severe shortage of electricity, at a time when we are using more of it than ever before. Green energy is nothing like as efficient as burning carbon. Indeed, the most efficient of all renewable technologies is the plant biomass combustion power station, which can have a load factor of 75%, although there is stern debate as to whether growing trees in order to burn them actually counts as carbon-neutral, particularly as the trees are generally transported to the power station by lorry.

The UK is increasingly reliant on renewable energy sources. Helpfully, average wind speeds tend to be higher in the winter, when the nation's solar generation is lower due to the shorter days and gloomy skies.

The trouble is that all of this new wind and solar electricity generation is "low inertia." In the good old days, a coal fired power station would contain one or more massive turbines. It would take an enormous amount of energy to start them turning, but once they were spinning they would carry on generating electricity even if there was a temporary interruption to the supply of energy to them within the power station.

This meant that the National Grid could reliably predict exactly how much electricity, and at exactly what voltage, each power station would produce on any given day. It was an extremely sensible system and had been designed to ensure that the lights stayed on in our homes, even if it meant that vast amounts of electricity were being generated overnight when nobody needed it, and huge amounts of carbon was released into the atmosphere.

In complete contrast, wind turbines are designed to be as light as possible, enabling them to commence generation in the gentlest of breezes. The result of this is that the turbine will spin at varying speeds throughout the day and will suddenly stop as soon as the wind stops. Solar panels are even worse; the sun is either shining or is not; electricity is generated accordingly.

This makes it very difficult for the National Grid to plan exactly where its electricity will come from at any given moment. As a result of this, the National Grid is requiring an enormous oversupply of electricity, in order to ensure that there is always the right amount at the right time.

Consequently, National Grid ESO began offering contracts in January of 2021 to electricity generation companies for what they call Dynamic Containment and the use of Balancing Mechanisms. Electricity generation companies can earn revenues from both DC and BM systems. Without spending too much time on the subject, the National Grid needs to be able to store electricity each and every half hour in storage systems (part of the Balancing Mechanism) but must also be able to make instant decisions to divert electricity in and out of the systems to prevent changes in supply and voltage, whether a surge or a drop.

The upshot of this is that owners of battery storage facilities can now fully benefit from the UK energy market. In 2020, National Grid paid nearly £1.8m for balancing services, which was nearly 50% more than the previous year. More money in the market will mean more people looking to invest in that market, which in turn will mean more opportunities for land owners to participate in the energy balancing market.

Battery Storage

Once electricity has been produced, it needs to be used instantly, unless it can be stored in a battery. Through the use of battery systems, landowners can participate in the energy balancing market. The owners of such systems can now sell both the storage capacity and the dynamic containment capacity of the same system. Prices paid for the electricity contained in battery storage systems have never been higher.

While conveyancers are unlikely to need to become involved with the wholesale electricity market, it is worth knowing the basics of that market.

Developing EV fast charging stations on a commercial park will give it access to the medium voltage grid, thereby taking EV demand away from the residential low voltage grid while adding stress to the supply in commercial districts. EVs tend to be charged at the same time each day, in a very predictable pattern; most of us drive the same pattern of journeys each and every week. EV owners tend to trickle charge their cars at home over night, and then use a fast charger at the office during the day. This means that they use a predictable amount of daytime and a separate predictable amount of night-time electricity. The National Grid loves such predicable consumers.

If there is room on site, your client should strongly consider adding a battery storage facility, whether alongside an EV charging station or as part of a solar or wind farm. The batteries, which are housed in containers designed to fit on the back on an HGV trailer, compliment an EV charging scheme by adding additional electrical capacity, and smoothing out peaks in demand. Batteries compliment generation schemes by storing any surplus electricity until it is needed by the Grid.

This might enable your client to develop a larger facility than would otherwise be possible.

Indeed, why not just develop a battery storage scheme as a standalone facility? The batteries are large and unsightly, but perhaps there is a suitable location for them tucked round a corner of the development?

As part of an EV charging facility, the large batteries are charged up from the Grid overnight, ready to discharge into EVs when all the cars arrive at work in the morning, which may be before the nation's solar PV stations are in full swing. The batteries then re-charge during the day, so that they can assist with the evening peak, when all those EVs need to be topped up before the rush hour drive home.

The operator of a battery storage facility will receive a fluctuating price for the electricity, which is released back to the Grid, with payments on the basis of hourly pricing which rises and falls to reflect supply and demand on a minute by minute basis. Battery storage facilities are not electricity generators, so do not benefit from feed in tariffs or smart export guarantees (see below).

The landlord of a battery storage facility would expect to receive a fixed rent based on the export capacity, rather than a figure based on the electricity actually exported.

A typical figure would be £2,000 per MW of export capacity per annum plus VAT. The larger the scheme, the larger the battery capacity, so the higher the rent. Such rent should be subject to a periodic review – very often you will see an annual rent review to capture changes in the Consumer Prices Index, with a five yearly open market review in order to capture changes in the market place, in each case on an upwards only basis.

The lease would typically run for a period of 25-35 years, only commencing when the tenant has obtained a satisfactory planning permission. You would therefore generally expect to see an option agreement, requiring the tenant to apply both for a grid connection and for planning permission.

Battery storage leases will contain funder Direct Agreements, very much in the form discussed above.

As we will see with solar and wind projects, any lease for a battery storage site should include a decommissioning bond. Most business leases include a requirement on the tenant to "make good". As the operators in the renewable energy sector tend to be new companies or SPVs with limited covenant strength, the landlord should require a bond to be provided to cover the cost of remediation. The bond should either be provided before the lease commences, or after ten years. If the tenth anniversary arrives without the bond being put in place, the landlord can forfeit and take control of the facility when it is still in good working order.

The clause might look like this:

> *"Prior to the Energisation Date, the Tenant must provide to the Landlord an in default bond or guarantee from a London clearing bank or substantial insurance company or trade association (in either case to be approved by the Landlord, such approval not to be unreason-ably withheld or delayed) in a form to be approved by the Landlord, such approval not to be unreasonably withheld or delayed to secure the performance by the Tenant of its obligations under this Lease, such bond or guarantee to be for an initial sum of £200,000 (such sum to be reviewed in accordance with Clause 10) ("the Decommissioning Sum"), and ensure that a bond or guarantee shall be in place (if*

so required) for the duration of this Lease and for the duration of any Decommissioning Period.

The Decommissioning Sum shall be subject to review one each fifth anniversary of the Term so that the Decommissioning Sum shall represent the cost of the works required during the Decommissioning Period and in the event of dispute either party may require the matter to be referred to Expert Determination.

This clause envisages that the site clearance might take place after the end of the term, with the tenant returning to site under licence.

The tenant would expect to pay half rent during the decommissioning period, whether it is during the fixed term or during a subsequent licence period. Equally, a half rent concession might be demanded during any period of initial works, before the site is switched on, or "energised".

As with all the leases discussed in this book the battery storage facility will need easements to enable a connection to the Grid and may also require a substation as well.

Earlier this year, the UK's largest battery was completed in Thurcroft, South Yorkshire, bringing 75MWh of energy storage to the Grid. If the rental value is anything like the figures discussed above, that will be a significantly valuable asset.

Nationally, there is currently more than 3GW of battery storage capacity in the UK with a further 4GW under construction and an astonishing 80GW at various stages of planning. Given the demands of grid balancing and dynamic containment, there is plenty of demand for more battery storage facilities.

Turning back briefly to electric cars, one of the key technologies will be V2G. Each of those hundreds of thousands of EVs contain a large and sophisticated battery. If every EV was plugged in everytime it was parked, rather than just when the owner wanted to charge it up, then the National Grid could benefit from millions of Watts of storage capacity, much of it right in the middle of busy towns and cities where electrical power is most needed. Using smart metering, and flexible tariffs, EV owners could leave their cars' onboard computers to decide whether or not to draw power from the network to charge the battery, or to send power from the battery to the grid. On a dull day, or a windless afternoon, EV batteries could provide vital back up power for the grid just when it is often needed most – at the start of a working day or in the early evening.

The UK is the world's fourth largest manufacturer of EV batteries. However, despite the opening of the taxpayer funded UK Battery Industrialisation Centre (UKBIC) near Coventry in 2021, this country lags a very long way behind China and the USA. Without a good supply of batteries, the green energy revolution might struggle to succeed.

Hydrogen

One of the key drivers in the current energy market is the need to produce too much electricity. Such an over capacity will allow the Grid to provide a more stable supply to our homes, given the problems of low inertia mentioned previously. Further, an over capacity will enable the efficient production of hydrogen.

The most plentiful substance in the universe, hydrogen is extremely easy to use as a fuel. It is currently transported in heavy pressurised cylinders, at great cost, but it is entirely feasible to transport it by pumping it through our existing gas pipeline network.

Oil and gas platforms are traditionally powered by on-site gas turbines which burn significant amounts of fuel and therefore cause significant emissions. In order to meet net zero goals, the oil and gas industry is therefore looking at alternative ways to electrify platforms. Given that a number of offshore wind farms are in close proximity to offshore oil and gas platforms, this presents opportunities for the use of offshore wind. There are some regulatory issues to resolve. The Oil & Gas Authority has pointed out that gas platforms are regulated by the Petroleum Act 1998, but an electric platform would come under the Energy Act 2008, which enables the Secretary of State to require a electricity generating company to deliver a specified quantity of renewable electricity to the Grid.

A new set of regulations is therefore needed.

Offshore wind can also generate electricity that can be converted to hydrogen via electrolysis of seawater. The hydrogen can then be pumped to shore via the existing gas pipelines – an offshore windfarm produces electricity which is used to create hydrogen, which is then pumped to shore using "second hand" gas pipes, rather than having to lay miles of new high voltage electrical cables.

The hydrogen can then either be stored or can be mixed with the existing "natural gas" (which is methane blended with propane and a little butane and ethane) and pumped directly into our homes. Cadent is currently trialling this with its Keele University HyDeploy project, which blends 20% hydrogen into the gas network. It seems to work, with no major engineering works required, although any cracks in the existing pipe network will be exposed; hydrogen is famously easy to ignite but actually is fairly low in "calories", so it has to be pumped at a higher pressure in order to ensure that my Sunday dinner does not take longer to cook.

Hydrogen works, and may well be the Next Big Thing, although many engineers think that the process is so complicated that it is easier just to generate and use electricity than to mess around with hydrogen.

Wind Turbines

On 6 October 2020, Prime Minister Boris Johnson speaking at the Conservative Party conference said:

> "Your kettle, your washing machine, your cooker, your heating, your plug-in electric vehicle – the whole lot of them will get their juice cleanly and without guilt from the breezes that blow around these islands."

The UK was to become the "Saudi Arabia of wind." He also stated that he would spend £160 million to upgrade ports and factories for building wind turbines and raised the target for offshore wind power capacity from 30 gigawatts to 40 gigawatts by 2030.

On 21st May 2021, the National Grid reported that 62.5% of Britain's electricity was being generated by wind power. However, this enormous figure was just for the one-hour period from 2am; even the UK's huge offshore wind farms are weather-dependent, meaning that supply can be interrupted by a lack of wind. At the time of writing in 2024, the figure was 49%, backed up by a mix of gas, nuclear, biomass and solar, with about 10% imported from France, Belgium, the Netherlands and Norway. The UK is the world leader in the development of floating windfarms. As the name suggests, floating windfarms actually float – each turbine stands on the top of a giant float. They can operate in deeper waters and will be particularly useful in the development of a domestic hydrogen supply, as mentioned above. The floating windfarm off the coast of Peterhead in Aberdeenshire has a load factor of approaching 60%; floating windfarms will definitely be part of the UK's energy mix as the years go by.

While offshore wind farms may grab the headlines, they are a little outside the scope of this book. Onshore wind farms are also worth looking at.

Wind turbines – planning issues

In England and Wales, on-shore wind turbines require planning permission.

The UK Government turned against onshore wind turbines when it introduced tough planning restrictions in 2015; the UK had plenty of electricity and did not want any more turbines. Changes to the electricity auction scheme, the Contracts for Difference, effectively ended onshore wind generation. However, the Government had a change of heart. In the autumn of 2023, planning regulations were changed such that local planning authorities were expected to approve planning applications for an onshore wind farm if:

(a) It is an area identified as suitable in the local development plan (local plan or a neighbourhood plan) or a supplementary planning document; and

(b) The planning impacts identified by the affected local community have been appropriately addressed and the proposal has community support.

This might best be described as a softening of Government hostility, rather than its heartfelt support. Nonetheless, these new regulations once again make onshore windfarms feasible. We will have to wait and see how many developers have sufficient confidence to return to this sector.

The smallest wind turbines may be classed as 'permitted development', for which planning permission is not required if the bottom of the blades are at least five metres off the ground.

If the turbine is to be pole-mounted, then the maximum height is 11.1m above the ground. Put another way, each turbine blade must be no more than 3 metres long, mounted 8 metres from the ground.

If the turbine is mounted to a building (which is quite unusual), for it to be classed as permitted development, then it must not protrude more than 3m above the roof, with a maximum height of 15m above the ground. This only applies to detached buildings; for any other building a full planning application will be required.

For permitted development rights to apply, there must be no other wind turbine or air source heat pump on the property, and the turbine site must not be in a Conservation Area, World Heritage site, or in the grounds of a listed building.

Any free-standing turbine must be at least 1.1 times of its own height away from the edge of the landowner's land, for obvious reasons.

As we saw with the use of permitted development rights for EV charging points, when a turbine which was erected using PD rights ceases to be used to generate electricity, it must be taken down.

An 11m wind turbine is a large structure but is small for a wind turbine. In a typical year, it should generate around 15,000kWh of power, which equates very roughly to 2kW at any given time. Given that onshore turbines have a load factor of around 20%, your 11m turbine might create a peak load closer to 10kW, but on average a typical 11m turbine should be able to power your fridge, freezer and electric iron, but would only cope with your washing machine spin cycle if the wind was blowing a gale or if you could call on reserve power from a battery storage facility.

Anything larger than this, will require a full planning application. Despite the changes to the subsidy scheme (of which, more below), planning permission remains very difficult to obtain.

The turbine must be in an area designated in the Local Plan, which is a planning process controlled by local government and therefore subject to local sensitivities.

If your client's site is in a designated area, before a planning permission can be made, the applicant must have addressed all local community concerns, so that it can be said to have their backing. This is a very tough hurdle to clear and has effectively stifled the development of on-shore turbines for several years.

Whether or not you agree with these two tests, the third test is difficult to argue with. At the site of each proposed turbine, the wind speed at 45m above ground level must be at least 5m/s. If this is not evidenced, then the application for planning will be refused.

The Government used to publish a list known as the NOABL database. This cumbersome acronym is short for the hefty phrase "numerical objective analysis of boundary layer" and represented the official database which mapped wind speeds for the entire country at 45m above ground level. The official NOABL database has now been scrapped, although a private organisation is attempting to maintain it; an internet search will reveal pages of very useful data. However, the private database carries no official weight, so your client can use the database for initial research but will then have to commission a specialist on-site survey.

Wind turbines – land law issues

While small turbines might be attached to a building or might stand on a simple concrete base, being held up by stay-wires, any turbine of any size will require a deep foundation. As we discussed earlier, this is where you might come into conflict with the owner of any mining or mineral rights. Such entries in the Proprietorship Register of a Land Registry title are often ignored as quaintly historic, but they can very much come to life as soon as the freeholder starts to dig and lay foundations. Such foundations will prevent the owner of the mineral rights from extracting those minerals (even if planning permission for their extraction would not foreseeably be granted). As with more mainstream developments, it is possible to obtain a policy of indemnity insurance to protect against any claim for infringement of mining and mineral rights. This issue should not be overlooked.

In addition, turbine blades may be considered to impact upon reserved right of sport (i.e. – the shooting of birds).

Large turbines can interfere with the flight paths of birds to protected nature reserves. The locations of local bird reserves should be easy enough to identify, but you will need specialist advice to ascertain whether or not your proposed turbine impacts upon the migration routes of passing bats. In either case, the turbines may need to be moved if planning permission is to be granted.

Your client may receive objections to the planning application from the RAF, if low-level flying takes place in that area, or from the Civil Aviation Authority if there is an airport in the vicinity. Such concerns can sterilise surprisingly large areas of land.

As with all planning applications, remember that an archaeological report is likely to be needed, which could take a significant time and cause considerable expense, depending on the size of the site.

Planning applications for larger wind turbines are likely to require the developer to agree to a clean-up regime which will be inserted into the planning permission as a condition. Such conditions are less commonly seen in planning permissions for solar farms.

Taking all of the above into account, the relatively simple task of erecting a medium sized wind turbine will require a large number of costly surveys and investigations before any electricity can be generated.

Regardless of the size of your client's proposed wind turbine, please remember that every large wind turbine actually needs electricity to operate. The turbine blades may be heated, to prevent damage from winter ice, and the blades are generally "trimmed" to the wind by electric motor. Further, the whole turbine is turned into the wind by an electric motor – they don't just "flap around" like the small turbines installed on the back of a canal boat. And, on very windy days, the turbine is switched off to protect it from storm damage, but the blades can be seen to be turning very slowly; an electric motor is turning the blades to protect against damage in extremely strong winds.

All of this means that your client needs to ensure that there is a power supply to the turbine as well as a connection from it to the Grid. With a large-scale connection, then this should not be a problem. However, with a medium sized installation designed only to supply your client's own premises, the need to supply the turbine with electricity might be overlooked. It can be a costly error.

Rent – how much rent will your client receive? If the turbine site is leased to a third-party operator, then the rent will typically be linked to the number of watts of electricity generated. The simplest calculation for the landlord is for the manufacturer's maximum output for each turbine to be multiplied by the usual load factor of 20% for an onshore turbine. That figure will provide the assumed average output in kWh, which can then be multiplied by the agreed figure to produce an annual rent. Current figures may be in the region of £2,000 to £3,000 per kWh per annum.

Some landlords might prefer to charge a rent based on the electricity actually generated. However, this puts the risk of calm days onto the landlord's shoulders.

The answer is to have a rent based on the assumed average output, with a profit rent in addition if the actual output exceeds a given threshold.

Rents would typically be subject to review each year based on increases in the Consumer Prices Index, with a further review every five years to catch increases in market values.

However, the assessment of rent is a specialist area, so having discussed these basic assumptions with your client, it is best to step back and leave the experts to agree the final figure.

Security of Tenure – at present, there is no special protection for wind turbine leases. This seems increasingly illogical, given the protection that is bestowed upon telecom masts. However, I hear no talk of a change in the law, so as matters stand wind turbine leases are just like any other business tenancy – they benefit from security of tenure under the Landlord and Tenant Act 1954, unless the necessary statutory declaration is made by the tenant to exclude security of tenure. Please remember however, as we discussed with EV charging stations, your client is likely to have to sign a wayleave or a freehold transfer for a substation, which makes the installation rather more permanent!

Wind turbines are large. It may seem an obvious point but does your client need any additional rights of access in order to get such large equipment and the associated lifting gear onto the site. While there are specialist haulage contractors who can solve all sort of issues such as arranging the removal of highway road signs, so that their huge lorries can get past, if your client needs the permission of a neighbour before an oversized lorry can swing into the site, then this needs to be addressed sooner rather than later.

Do your client's title deeds prohibit the causing of nuisance? While it is likely that any party who will be affected by the noise produced by your new wind turbines will already have made a complaint as part of the planning process, the issue of nuisance should not be overlooked. Even the quietest of turbines do produce noise, for this reason, most sites are located either in very remote spots or near to major roads – there is either no neighbour to complain, or the noise of the turbine is drowned out by the background drone of passing traffic.

The Impact of Off-shore wind to On–shore landowners.

At some point, all that off-shore electricity has to come on-shore.

In February 2021, the small village of Necton near Swaffham in the west of Norfolk hit the headlines in the legal press. Necton is 40 miles from the sea, and yet it is the centre of the off-shore electricity industry in the East Anglia region.

Currently, the Necton substation services the Dudgeon Offshore Wind Farm, which stands 20 miles off the coast near to Cromer. The substation at Necton is therefore about 60 miles from the wind turbines. According to the owners of the Dudgeon windfarm, the cable passes through the property of 44 different landowners at a depth of 1.4metres, while the substation itself can handle more than 400MW of electricity.

Necton substation is also crucial to the development of two huge new windfarms due to be built off the coast of Norfolk near to Great

Yarmouth, known as Boreas and Vanguard. Campaigners in Necton have successfully held up these huge infrastructure projects.

Necton itself will benefit very little from the windfarms – specialist labour will build the new substation facility, while will then be largely unstaffed. But, Necton will have to endure the huge trenches that are dug for the enormous cables. The developers have promised to fill the trenches in and restore the area to its former natural beauty, but this process will take years. Each wind farm, indeed each individual turbine would require a separate connection to the substation, resulting in huge amount of excavation in the Necton area.

Planning permission is required for each individual cable from the point that it reaches the shore. This would be a matter for the local planning authority in the case of a small windfarm, but the Necton cables were national infrastructure, so, the developer made an application to the Planning Inspectorate for a Development Consent Order, as permitted by the Planning Act 2008.

The Secretary of State for Business granted a Development Consent Order for the scheme, but the High Court held on 18th February 2021 that this DCO had not fully taken account of the disruption to visual amenity to the people in the Necton area.

The Court heard arguments about whether or not it was possible to consolidate all these cables offshore, beneath the waves. Argument was given that the technology does not yet exist for such a high voltage under-sea grid. None of this impressed the Court – the DCO needed to be revisited.

The Court held that the lengthy disruption needed to have been considered more fully. The first of the two windfarms has been halted, while an identical complaint against the second windfarm remains to be heard, but will presumably provide the same outcome.

Almost exactly one year later In February 2022, the Secretary of State confirmed the DCO, giving the green light to the huge Vanguard scheme. The Boreas scheme will presumably also be granted consent. In the end, the objectors were not successful, but landowners will have taken note that even the largest schemes can be brought to a halt if the electricity cable to the substation cannot be laid!

The case of People Over Wind

The People Over Wind case may not appear immediately relevant. It concerned the application of EU regulations to the laying of cables for an off-shore wind farm in Ireland. The initial assessment showed that the cable works could release silt into the water, which would harm the mussel fisheries.

In April 2018, the Court of Justice of the European Union delivered its judgment in Case C-323/17 People Over Wind & Peter Sweetman v Coillte Teoranta ('People over Wind'). The judgment clarified that when making screening decisions for the purposes of deciding whether an appropriate assessment is required, competent authorities cannot take into account any mitigation measures.

This means that a competent authority can only take account of mitigation measures intended to avoid or reduce the harmful effects of a plan or project as part of an appropriate assessment itself.

UK case law had previously allowed mitigation measures to be taken into account at the initial screening stage. It was held in the People Over Wind case that the initial screening is not the appropriate time for the consideration of all the required environmental measures but should be part of the later Environmental Impact Assessment.

The EIA may require mitigation measures to avoid or reduce any adverse effects that may be caused by the proposed project to the local environment, such the use of a less damaging method of construction or carrying out works outside a breeding season. The mitigation measures may even require parts of the project to be abandoned.

The upshot of all of this is that any major renewable energy scheme will need to comply with the tightened regulations regarding mitigation measures. Even though the UK has left the EU, mitigation measures must be investigated as part of the detailed EIA, rather than as part of the initial screening assessment. Further costs for the landowner, but hopefully, further protection for the environment.

Wind Micro-Generation

The portable turbine used by some camping enthusiasts has come of age. With a single vertical "spiral" blade, such turbines are remarkably efficient at capturing low wind speeds. New equipment is coming to the market every year, and in 2021 the owners of the O2 Arena announced that they were installing a series of vertical turbines on the roof stays of the famous London dome, with the manufacturers also hoping to install their turbines onto motorway lighting poles.

Microgeneration produces small quantities of electricity, but there are many more potential locations for these small turbines. Perhaps this too will form part of the future?

Anaerobic digestion

Anaerobic digesters, or AD Plants as they tend to be known, are an excellent way for farms and rural businesses to diversify, and to protect themselves against rising energy prices.

An AD plant is basically a large tank full of organic matter. As there is virtually no air in the tank, the material decays "anaerobically" and produces the greenhouse gas methane. In a garden compost heap, this is very bad, but the AD plant turns it to an advantage. The methane is drawn off in a pipe and burned.

The resultant heat is either used by the farmer to warm his or her buildings or is put to use in an electricity generation plant – as with those old gas fired power stations, the heat causes water to boil, and the steam makes a turbine spin. The spinning turbine generates electricity.

Occasionally, the methane gas is piped off, filtered and pumped directly into the national gas grid, but this would require the farm to be located immediately adjacent to major gas pipes.

Focusing on those AD plants which produce electricity, the issues are very similar to those which we have seen with the other technologies referred to in this book.

A typical small farm which signs a lease for an ADP plant may expect to receive rent or perhaps £30,000 to £50,000 per annum over a 25-year period. The farm owner will need to consider all of the issues discussed above regarding cable easements and the location of a substation. The documentation will also probably contain a requirement that the farm owner enters into a direct agreement with a funding party at some point in the future. Decommissioning agreements backed by security bonds are also important, as we have discussed earlier in this book.

The bigger issue with AD plants is contained in a separate agreement referred to as an "feedstock contract".

The organic material that goes into the digestion tank might be post-consumer waste, or food waste that never reached the supermarket shelves in the first place. More commonly, the organic matter will be a cash crop grown specifically for the purpose. Many of the fields of maize which we see in the English countryside are destined to be harvested and fed directly into an AD digester.

The trouble for the conveyancing solicitor is that the business case for the AD plant depends entirely upon the business case for the feedstock agreement, but the farm owner is quite likely already to have signed the feedstock agreement on the basis that this is a simple farming contract. However, unless the income stream in both contracts adds up to the correct sum, the farm owner will end up signing long term contracts which don't make financial sense.

The feedstock agreement will require that the farmer delivers certain tonnage of good quality dry feedstock each month. The price for the feedstock may be fixed for years in advance, with an annual review to reflect changes in RPI/CPI. This provides a certainty of income but removes from the farm owner any ability to react to significant changes in farm gate prices over the period of the contract.

The duty to dry the feedstock falls on the farm owner. Vague promises may have been made about the surplus heat generated by the AD plant being made available for the drying of feedstock, but is this documented anywhere? If the feedstock is not dry, then the operator of the AD plant will reject it.

The lease for the AD plant will document the rent that is to be paid and will confirm who owns the electricity that is generated by the plant. However, has anyone thought to document who owns the slurry which gathers at the bottom of the AD tank, which periodically has to be emptied out and thrown away? This slurry is enormously valuable as farmyard compost, and the farm owner can find it particularly galling to see a neighbouring farmer drive up his lane and collect slurry from his AD plant.

If the slurry is to belong to your farming client at the end of the process, then the lease should specify this in no uncertain terms. The feedstock contract may state that it is an annual contract, easily terminable by either party.

However, the AD plant lease might state that the operator can terminate the AD plant lease if the feedstock agreement falls away. More commonly, the AD plant lease might allow the operator to terminate in the event that the AD plant becomes economically unviable. If your farmer client threatens to terminate a feedstock agreement which is losing him money on each tonne of maize that leaves the farm gate, then the AD plant operator will simply threaten to terminate the AD plant lease. Your client might have already got in rather too deep before you even get to see the documents.

Gas Reserve Power Stations

One of the more surprising elements of the renewable energy network is the gas reserve power station. Often referred to as a "gas gen-sets", the UK has a growing network of small gas-fired power stations dotted around the nation, which can be switched on at a moment's notice if there is a drop in electricity supply or a sudden boom in demand. Put simply, they are very small gas power stations, or very large kettles! Each unit is delivered on the back of a lorry and occupies the space of a standard shipping container. Looking therefore rather like a battery storage unit, the tell-tale difference is the large chimney/funnel on top for the steam and gas vapour to escape.

Gas gen-sets are in no way "green" but they are a vital part of the green energy network. Traditional full-size gas power stations take days to heat up to operational temperature, whereas a small gen-set will be active within minutes. They are switched on and off remotely and supply their electricity into the National Grid.

If your client has a small parcel of land which is located close to both a substantial gas main and to high voltage electricity lines, but is otherwise not obviously developable, then this might be a development that is worth considering.

All the issues which we have discussed above regarding remediation bonds and direct agreements apply to gas reserve power stations. The tenancy will be subject to the security of tenure provisions of the Landlord and Tenant Act 1954 in the same way as the other leases we have discussed, and the tenant is highly likely to require easements and wayleaves for electricity cables and gas pipes and may require a new substation as well.

When agreeing the rent, it is usual for the figure to be agreed based on the maximum electricity generation capacity of the equipment which has been given planning permission and installed. Rental values of course vary, but it would be no surprise to see a figure of £4,000-£5,000 for each MW of capacity installed. Please note that it is very easy for the tenant/developer to increase this capacity – you simply bring onto the site another gen-set and connect it to the equipment installed at the beginning of the lease. Therefore, the rent should increase with any increase in capacity. As you would expect, this rental figure should be reviewed annually in accordance with any increase in the relevant index, with a periodic open market review as well.

As for the drafting of the lease, look out for some of the following points:

> *"Equipment" means the electrical generation plant, cooling radiators and associated equipment detailed in the schedule to this lease together with all subsidiary machinery apparatus or items reasonably required for the operation and use of it as the same may be altered, varied or substituted from time to time in*

> *accordance with clause 3.9 and as initially shown on the attached plan;*
>
> *"Permitted Use" means use for electricity generation and associated services and any other uses that fall within classes B1(C), B2 and B8 of the Town and Country Planning (Use Clauses Order) Act 1987 (as amended);*
>
> *The Tenant shall yield and deliver up the Property to the Landlord on determination of the Lease (however that occurs) free from any third party occupations and to remove the Equipment and any Buildings and make good to the reasonable satisfaction of the Landlord any damage whatsoever caused by the removal of the Equipment and the Buildings and make safe the Property all such reinstatement works to be done in accordance with practices, methods and procedures which would be adopted by a skilled and experienced operator of the Permitted Use acting in accordance with all legal obligations provided always that the Landlord by written notice to the Tenant may require the Tenant to leave in situ any fencing and/or concrete plinths or hardstanding areas.*

Ideally, the Landlord will obtain a remediation bond from the tenant, but otherwise it will need to rely on a standard yielding up clause such as:

> *If the Tenant does not comply with its obligations in this clause, then, without prejudice to any other right or remedy of the Landlord, the Tenant shall pay the Landlord an amount equal to the Rent at the rate reserved immediately before the end of the term for the period that it would reasonably take to put the Property into the condition it would have been in had the Tenant performed its obligations under this clause. The amount shall be a debt due on demand from the Tenant to the Landlord.*

The Tenant shall not make any alteration, addition or improvement to the Property (save for those works specified in the schedule to this lease unless the Tenant has:

- *submitted to the Landlord detailed plans and specifications showing the proposed works;*
- *obtained and supplied copies to the Landlord of all Necessary Consents to carry out the proposed works;*
- *given to the Landlord such covenants relating to the carrying out of the proposed works as the Landlord may reasonably require; and*
- *has obtained the Landlord's consent to the works such consent not to be unreasonably withheld;*

The Tenant may make any improvements or alterations to the Equipment and may lay, install, use, supplement, upgrade or replace the Equipment and any Service Media exclusively serving the Equipment in all cases without obtaining the Landlord's consent provided that such works do not increase the footprint of the Equipment, nor alter the Equipment's principal function from the generation of electricity.

As we have seen elsewhere, the tenant's funder may or may procure the tenant to assign or novate the Lease, requiring the landlord to enter into a direct agreement.

The Tenant may assign the whole of the Property to the Funder where the Funder is exercising any step in rights that the Funder has the benefit of pursuant to any facility agreement or other funding arrangement and if it has received notice pursuant to this Lease and has undertaken to remedy any outstanding breach of covenant within a reasonable period of time provided that the Funder has first demonstrated to the reasonable satisfaction of the Landlord that it will be reasonably capable of complying with the Tenant's covenants under this Lease.

As we discussed in relation to electricity charging lease works compounds, the construction of the site might require the tenant to occupy some of the landlord's adjoining land. The demised site needs to be flat and level, so it may be necessary for the tenant to move earth around. If your landlord client has suitable adjoining land, then you might wish to agree a clause like this:

Any topsoil removed from the Landlord's Estate as part of the Tenant's Works is to be delivered to the Landlord at a single tipping location on the Landlord's Estate to be agreed between the parties each acting reasonably. The parties acknowledge that the Landlord will accept responsibility for any soil so delivered. The Landlord's Estate is to be left level tidy and in a clean condition following completion of the Tenant's Works.

Solar Panels (Photovoltaic – PV Panels)

Many landlords will seek to gain an extra income stream by installing solar panels on the rooftops of their building, whether a small agricultural unit or a huge distribution warehouse.

The principals we have discussed above will apply to solar panels in much the same way as they apply to wind turbines or indeed EV charging stations; the landowner will need to enter into a fairly long-term lease, typically having granted an option agreement / agreement for lease first in order to allow the developer to bring its scheme together. If the PV panels are to be installed on the roof of the tenant's building, then the landlord will need to consider an application for licence to carry out alterations.

What is the position regarding planning permission? Are PD rights available? Under the terms of The Town and Country Planning (General Permitted Development) (Amendment) (England) Order 2015, permitted development rights are available for the installation, alteration or replacement of PV equipment on residential buildings, and outbuildings which are within the residential curtilage. There are strict limitations – permitted development rights are not available on residential buildings if the PV or solar thermal equipment would protrude more than 20 centimetres beyond a wall or the roof slope or if the PV panels protrude above the roof line.

The same basic principles apply to PD rights for PV arrays on commercial buildings, but the panels must not come within 1m of the edge of the roof space.

Ground based PV arrays also benefit from PD rights, but only if the scheme does not exceed 9 sqm in total. Most of the solar farms which come across a conveyancer's desk will be significantly larger than this, and therefore outside the scope of PD rights.

As we have seen already, any equipment which is installed using PD rights must be removed once it has ceased to be used. A landlord might therefore prefer to require that its tenant obtained a formal planning permission, rather than relying on PD rights, in order to avoid a potential problem with the planning enforcement officer in the event that the building becomes vacant for a protracted period.

The issue of business rates has been of great concern in recent years. In 2021, a temporary change to the business rates regime was introduced, to run from 2023 to 2035. This temporary regime removed non-domestic rooftop solar panels from business rates altogether – although they will be brought back into account in 2036.

This temporary regime was introduced following a backlash against the Government's 2017 changes to business rates. Before 2017, business rates had been payable at a flat rate of £8/kW but this was scrapped and new charges were introduced to try to encourage building owners to export more electricity to the Grid. From 2017, businesses which exported more than 50% of the electricity generated by their PV arrays benefitted from a lower business rates bill where the rateable value is assessed on the basis of the costs and expenditure incurred.

Conversely, businesses that exported less than 50%, had to pay more business rates payable at a multiplier of 0.504 giving a rateable Value of approximately £50/kW.

The major supermarket chain Lidl, which had been at the vanguard of rooftop PV generation, saw a 500% increase in its business rates bill due to this 2017 revaluation of its rooftop solar panels. The problem for Lidl was that it used these PV arrays to power its supermarkets and distribution hubs, rather than exporting the electricity to the Grid. It therefore saw a huge increase in its business rates bill. Given that all the major supermarket chains have significant rooftop PV capacity (indeed, they are owners of a very large amount of roof space), this problem must have been faced by other major retailers as well as Lidl.

Immediately, owners of large rooftops started investigating systems whereby they supplied neighbouring third-party rooftops, rather than their own roofs, in order to benefit from the more benign business rates treatment for exported electricity.

Commonsense prevailed and the Chancellor, one Rishi Sunak, introduced business rates relief up until 2035. However, the fundament problem remains, unless the underlying rating system is also changed. Will investors be comfortable relying on a temporary relief?

Small business owners benefitted from 100% relief for assessments under £12,000 for the total solar equipment owned by that specific company. As far as business rates are concerned, "solar" also includes solar thermal panels, which generate hot water rather than electricity. Such systems are generally small scale and are otherwise outside the scope of this book.

Business rates are of course not payable on PV arrays installed on dwelling houses, although please be aware of schemes which can turn a household rooftop into a business – if the airspace immediately above the roof is let to a PV developer, then that area will arguably be a separate business premises, and therefore subject to business rates and also likely to benefit from security of tenure. If your client is seeking to carry out such a residential rooftop scheme, please be aware that this is almost certainly going to be a breach of any standard residential mortgage.

There are also special rules which apply to farms. Farms, which are exempt from general business rates, are also exempt from business rates on PV arrays if the farm uses more than 90% of the power generated. This is fine as long as the PV array is designed to supply the farm, with perhaps a little space capacity to bring in some useful additional income. However, if the solar array is later extended, the farm might fall outside of this 10% / 90% threshold. Suddenly, business rates are payable on the whole array on the same basis as a supermarket pays for its rooftop PV array. This business rates trap can be factored into any plans to expand the solar equipment, and the farmer's accountant can check to see if the figures make the expansion worthwhile. Please note however that the farm owner can also get caught if the farm itself becomes more energy efficient, or if the farm diversifies away from farming – suddenly the 90% threshold might not be met, even though no additional capacity has been created.

Power Purchase Agreements

Power purchase agreements (PPAs) deserve a book all to themselves, but it is important to introduce them here.

If your client is the landlord of a commercial anaerobic digester or biomass plant, or indeed of premises with rooftop solar equipment, the developer tenant might pay a fully commercial rent for the facility. Alternatively, the tenant might pay a notional rent and then offer an attractive PPA as a collateral contract.

The PPA will state that the tenant must offer electricity to the landlord, at a given price. This price should be sufficiently attractive to compensate the landlord for the lack of rent on the demised premises. Typically, the rent will be at a percentage discount below market rent, but sometimes the figure will fixed. If so, then please strongly advise your clients to take independent advice as to the most suitable figure.

Depending on the complexity of the scheme, the key clauses can be fairly simple. I set out some wording below, where the Landlord is the Purchaser, and the Tenant is the Generator:

> *Energy Price – the charge for electricity supplied by the Generator to the Purchaser pursuant to this agreement in each Billing Period shall be the amount of kWh supplied in the relevant Billing Period multiplied by the Current Unit Price (being the Base Price multiplied by the Index on an annual basis.)*

The Generator shall supply electricity from the Equipment to the Purchaser at the electricity Delivery Point. The rate of electricity supply from the Generator to the Purchaser at any time shall be the lesser of:

(a) the Purchaser's demand for active power;

(b) the active power generated by the Equipment (less active power consumed in the operation of the Equipment); and

(c) the Maximum Capacity of the Equipment.

The Purchaser acknowledges and agrees that the supply of electricity by the Equipment is dependent on various factors, including weather conditions. The Generator therefore gives no warranty as to the amount of electricity which will be generated by the Equipment.

The Generator shall be free to export and sell to the Grid or sell any electricity generated by the Equipment which is not consumed by the Purchaser.

The PPA should be co-terminus with the lease of the premises.

If the consideration paid to the landlord is the sum of the rent for the demised premises and the discount achieved under the PPA, then it is essential that the two documents are inter-lined and co-terminus. It is also essential that the landlord carefully checks that the figures "work" – sometimes an overly generous rent can be used to disguise a disadvantageous PPA or vice versa. The two contracts must be read in conjunction with each other.

Solar Farms

For many landowner clients, the development of a greenfield solar farm is much more likely than creating a rooftop scheme.

Solar farms are typically huge. The larger the PV array, the more electricity will be generated, and therefore the more rent will be paid to the landowner.

Many schemes are designed to generate 49.9MW of electricity. There are two reasons for this: (i) the old feed-in tariff was a government scheme which supported energy projects but which did not apply to schemes of 50MW or more, and (ii) any energy project which generates 50 MW or more is classified as a Nationally Significant Infrastructure Project (NSIP). If you wish to develop and NSIP, your planning application goes to the Secretary of State who will issue a Development Consent Order, rather than going to the local planning authority for the grant of planning permission. The application system for an DCO is much more rigorous than for a planning permission, so developers will try to keep their schemes below the 50MW threshold if possible.

In 2023, the definition of a megawatt was changed by the government in the policy document EN3. The definition had previously been unclear as to whether a megawatt was DC or AC, but the assumption was that it was a reference to power in DC. In other words, a scheme could generate 50MW of power before being classified as a Nationally Significant Infrastructure Project. Since 2023 however, a megawatt is a megawatt of power AC. Remembering the loss of power in converting from DC to AC, this means that a scheme can generate approximately 65MW DC before It can deliver 50MW to the Grid. Schemes of around 65MW DC will therefore start to become more common, rather than being either capped at 49.9MW or being significantly larger.

When considering a new solar project, given that the solar farm will cover such a large area of land, the landowner should focus first and foremost on the reinstatement of the land at end of term. This seems a strange way to look at the scheme, but most solar farms are being built on farmland, and farmers tend to think very long term. The PV array may well only be in use for a generation, after which time the equipment might be out of date and in need of being scrapped and removed. This applies to all leases, but perhaps particularly in the case of these very large solar farms.

At the start of the lease term, the developer will have installed new roads, as well as underground cabling and hundreds of ground level PV panels.

At the end of the term, the tenant should be required to remove its equipment. This is also fairly standard landlord and tenant practice, but in the case of solar farms, the landlord may wish to limit its obligation to the removal of the above ground kit, while leaving all the below ground kit safely in place.

You might expect to see wording like this in the lease:

> *The Property will be reinstated to its current state by the tenant, or as agreed between the parties, at the end of the Lease, in accordance with the attached schedule of condition. The Tenant will not be liable to remove any Service Media which has been adopted by Statutory Undertakers, provided that any such wayleaves or easements or agreements with statutory undertakers shall include an appropriate lift and shift clause for future relocation.*
>
> *For the avoidance of doubt, Tenant must return the Property to the Landlord having removed all equipment installed by the Tenant on the Property including any part of any such*

> *equipment which is below ground level (except any Service Media serving the Property, equipment or structures which are entirely situated 1.0 metre or more below ground level or have been adopted by a statutory undertaker or are owned by an electricity distribution network operator or which cannot be removed as a condition of the Planning Consent or which would be a breach of statute or regulations) and must make good any damage caused as a result of the removal to the satisfaction of the Landlord acting reasonably. Any Service exclusively serving the Property, equipment or structures not removed must be made safe and be left in a safe condition.*

The purpose of this lengthy proviso about kit which is more than one metre below ground is to ensure that the tenant removes any concrete foundations which are at ground level, and which may also project down more than one metre, but that the tenant leaves in situ any cables which are buried deep in the soil – removing them would cause huge damage to the structure of the soil.

Solar farm leases tend to run for a period of 30 to 35 years. This is a little longer than is typical for EV charge point leases, as the equipment is assumed to last a little longer. The schedule of condition referred to above is important, but it must record the condition of the soil and any land drains so will be drawn up by an agricultural specialist rather than the building surveyor who might typically assist you with schedules of condition.

The provision of a remediation bond is important. If the tenant does not provide this bond, typically on the tenth anniversary, then the landlord can forfeit the lease while the equipment is still in a good and serviceable condition.

The Tenant will not be liable to remove any Service Media which has been adopted by Statutory Undertakers, provided that any such wayleaves or easements or agreements with statutory undertakers shall include an appropriate lift and shift clause for future relocation.

Earlier In this book, we discussed the need for a decommissioning bond. With solar farm leases, this is particularly important due to the long length of the lease term, and the sheer size of the scheme.

A typical clause reads as follows:

- *Prior to the 20th anniversary of the Commissioning Date, the Tenant shall instruct an independent professional (whose identity shall first be agreed by the parties both acting reasonably and expeditiously and who shall have Ie of developments similar to the Development) to review and provide a reasonable estimate of the costs of the Tenant complying with its decommissioning obligations, taking Into account the scrap value of any equipment and shall provide a copy of that estimate to the Landlord.*

- *Reinstatement Cost = [cost of clearing the site – scrap value of the kit].*

- *The Tenant shall on the 20th anniversary of such Commissioning Date put in place security in favour of the Landlord security for an amount equivalent to the Reinstatement Cost.*

This security might be paid in instalments of (e.g.) 20% in years 20 to 24.

As an alternative, here Is another clause which addresses the same issue:

- *Tenant shall on or prior to the tenth anniversary of this Lease place a sum equal to 100% of the Reinstatement Cost in a bond, insurance policy or bank guarantee as the Tenant acting reasonably may elect and as approved by the Landlord (such approval not to be unreasonably withheld or delayed) (the "Security") provided that:*

    - *Landlord may have recourse to the Security if and to the extent that the Tenant has failed to comply with its obligations under this lease;*

    - *the balance of the Security shall be repaid to the Tenant on the expiry or sooner determination of this Lease;*

    - *if a planning permission requires that similar security is put in place then these provisions relating to the Security shall not apply*

- *The Reinstatement Cost shall be reviewed on the 10th and 20th anniversaries of the Term Commencement Date and the relevant adjustment to the Reinstatement Cost shall be paid into the Security by the Tenant within 5 working days.*

How much rent will your client expect to earn? This is obviously a matter for your client's agent or estate manager, but please remember that PV panels typically have a load factor of around 11%. This means that the panels will typically generate only 11% of their advertised electrical capacity. If rent is paid on the basis of £/MW of capacity, then please be certain to find out whether this relates to the maximum capacity or the amount of electricity which will actually be generated in a typical year.

The developer might offer to pay rent on the basis of £/acre or £/watt generated, but the same principal applies – is the underlying calculation based on the potential maximum capacity or the typical capacity bearing in mind the 11% load factor.

Whichever rent is agreed, the tenant may well insist that it only pays half rent for the first year, and possibly also for the final year, as compensation for its fitting out and remediation costs.

Here is some useful wording for these reduced rental periods:

- *Construction Rent and Decommissioning Rent shall be 50% of the Base Rent*

- *From and including the Term Commencement Date until the day prior to the Commissioning Date, the Tenant shall pay to the Landlord the Construction Rent quarterly in advance on the Rent Payment Dates.*

- *From and including the Commissioning Date until the day prior to the Decommissioning Date the Tenant shall pay to the Landlord the Base Rent quarterly in advance on the Rent Payment Dates.*

- *From and including the Decommissioning Date up until the expiry of the term, the Tenant shall pay to the Landlord the Construction Rent quarterly in advance on the Rent Payment Dates.*

Another way of resolving the rent calculation is to require the tenant to pay a base rent of (for example) £1,000 per acre, with a further rent being 5% of the value of electricity actually generated.

Any base rent would then be subject to an annual rent review based on increases in the consumer price index, with a periodic open market review as well. In relation to the turnover rent, this would typically be based on the income actually received by the tenant for the sale of the electricity to the Grid. The figures would therefore fluctuate significantly, depending on the market price at any given time. As with any turnover rent, this will require the tenant to make full disclosure and for the parties to agree which sums may fairly be deducted from the tenant's income before calculating the rent due to the landlord. The percentage which is then due to the landlord will depend entirely on how high the base rent is.

While agreeing the rent for the site Is Important, don't forget the need to discuss rent for any land which is severed from the rest of the farm by the solar scheme. Should the developer/tenant be required to take this Severed Land for full rent, or is the tenant allowed to pay just agricultural rent for this land?

The same applies to land which Is required for any construction compound. Does the tenant pay full rent, or just a peppercorn, given that that the construction compound is essential for the development of the project?

Furthermore, solar schemes are now required to deliver an environmental enhancement to the local area, under the Biodiversity Net Gain regulations. All development projects must now deliver an element of BNG, either on site or by way of an off-site provision. Landlords of solar projects must decide if they can provide this BNG land within the "red line" of the solar lease, or if the BNG must be provided elsewhere. Either way, the BNG land will attract a rent – should it be a peppercorn, agricultural value or full development value? That Is a commercial decision for the parties to agree upon.

Similar to BNG is the issue of green credits. Since the UK's departure from the European Union, the old system of the Basic Payment Scheme has been closed and will finally be wound up In 2027, having been replaced by the environmental land management scheme. This is just one of many potential benefits and credits which are available to the landlord and tenant. The parties must agree who gets which benefit. Generally, anything which relates to the soil is passed to the landlord while anything which relates to the kit goes to the tenant. A clause like this might be useful:

- *Subject to the Landlord having provided the Company with details on the environmental land management scheme, basic payment scheme, countryside stewardship scheme or higher-level stewardship payments which affect the Property, the Company will compensate the Landlord for ELMS BPS, CSS and HLS up until Completion, such assessment to be in accordance with Central Association of Agricultural Valuers.*

- *The Tenant shall then pass to the Landlord all payments received which relate solely to the ground beneath the solar panels but without any obligation on the Tenant to apply for or secure such benefits. Any other green benefits received by the Tenant shall belong to the Tenant.*

Tenants will want to add a few storage batteries onto the site, If there Is room. Your landlord client might be happy with this, but batteries do attract a higher rent per acre than solar panels. Consider a user clause like this:

- *Permitted Use means the development, construction, repair, operation and decommissioning on the Premises of:*

  (i) photovoltaic cells and the frames supporting such photovoltaic cells and such ancillary equipment for the

purpose of the generation, distribution and supply of electricity; and/or

(ii) a battery storage facility less than or equal to 1MVa including storage containers, transformers, batteries and Conducting Media as is reasonably necessary for the purpose of storage of electricity and the distribution and supply of electricity.

This clause will place a cap on the number of large and unsightly batteries which can be Installed on the site but will not attract any additional rent. Alternatively, the landlord might allow batteries but require a separate rent:

- *Battery Storage Rent – £2,000/MW DC of storage capacity*

As discussed above in relation to EV Charge Points, the tenant may be required a break right. While most leases now have unconditional break rights, energy leases tend to require that the tenant has complied with its obligation to pay a decommissioning bond before any break may be exercised:

- *The Tenant may determine the Lease at any time during the Term by giving the Landlord not less than 12 months' prior written notice provided that on or before the expiration of any such notice (the Break Date) either:*
    - *the Tenant has paid the Decommissioning Costs into the Decommissioning Account; or*
    - *the balance of the Decommissioning Account has been released to the Tenant following the Tenant's compliance with the Decommissioning Obligations*

then this Lease will determine on the Break Date without prejudice to the rights of either party against the other for any antecedent breach of obligations under this Lease;

- *In the event that neither of the conditions under this clause are satisfied on or before the Break Date, the Break Date shall be postponed to such date as either of those conditions have been satisfied, upon which this Lease will determine.*

Solar farms are businesses, so the lease of the land will be subject to the security of tenure provisions of the Landlord and Tenant Act 1954. Remember also that the land being leased to the solar farm operator may well be currently tenanted.

Part of the deal for securing a surrender by the farm tenant will be the payment of a negotiated sum for crop loss. A suitable clause might look like this:

- *To minimise loss of crop on any arable land and pay reasonable compensation to the Landlord for any damage caused to the Landlord's Property caused by the exercise of the rights granted this Agreement which is not promptly made good by the Company. Any calculation of compensation for crop loss shall be assessed in accordance with Central Association of Agricultural Valuers.*

In days gone by, solar farms often allowed (or even required) the landlord farmer to continue to graze the ground between the panels. Large animals such as cattle and pigs would be prohibited, but sheep or even chickens might be allowed, in order to prevent the land from being infested with weeds. Remember, the farmer will want the land to be returned in a condition suitable for farming, in a generation's time. Modern solar farms are much more tightly packed with PV arrays, so grazing is often not possible. Even so, the tenant must still take steps to prevent soil loss and pernicious weeds and might be required to cover the ground with sheeting for the duration of the term.

The flagship scheme at Cleve Hill in Kent was granted planning permission by way of Development Consent Order in 2020 and has seen 900 acres of farmland being developed as a solar farm. The PV panels are very densely massed onto half of the site and are built on tall stilts to take them above the flood waters of the nearby river Swale. Due to this increased intensity, only half of the site is needed for PV arrays. The rest is being left as river wetlands, with a substantial new managed wetland being created by the developers. It is estimated that the 450 acres of PV panels will produce enough electricity to power more than 90,000 homes.

As we have discussed already, does this new scheme require a substation? All the principals we saw above very much apply to solar farms. As a further point, it may be that the solar farm is being developed as a "green bonus" for a major housing development in the locality? If so, your landowner client could insist that the substation is installed on the housing land, in order to avoid the problem that the substation will still be on site many years after the solar farm has been dismantled.

A solar farm tenant is almost certainly going to insist that the landlord agrees to sign a Direct Agreement, as we discussed earlier.

Before we finish with solar farms, there are a couple of additional clauses which every lease should contain. Farms need good soil, and no farmer will allow good soil to go to waste:

- *The right to deposit soil and other spoil from the construction, maintenance, repair, renewal and replacement of the Access, Equipment and the Development in such position or positions on the Landlord's Property and in such manner as the Landlord shall approve (including without limitation grading and seeding such soil or other spoil) (such approval not to be unreasonably withheld or delayed).*

The tenant needs strong sunlight, so this clause is seen in most solar farm leases:

- *The right to fell, lop, remove or cut any trees, shrubs, bushes, hedges or branches on the Premises which (if not lopped, felled or cut) would obstruct or interfere with the passage of solar irradiation to the Equipment.*

CHAPTER FIVE

GRANTS, SUBSIDIES AND TAX

Grant funding

The landlord can apply for a Government grant. The Government has put aside up to £1 billion, including a new £100 million fund for EV charging grants, to be administered by the Office for Zero Emission Vehicles (previously called the Office for Low Emission Vehicles).

The most obvious source of funding is the Workplace Charging Scheme, which provides vouchers to help with the cost of installing EV charging points, to be used by any business with off-street parking for employee use. Businesses can apply for financial assistance with up 40 charge-point sockets, which must be installed by a Government approved contractor within 180 days of the date of the voucher.

The grant will cover up to 75% of the cost of buying and fitting the charging points, capped at £350 for each socket. The idea is to assist companies with the installation of the most widely useful types of charging station, so that the widest possible group of employees can use them, not just the Chief Executive with a brand-new Tesla. The scheme clearly envisages the installation of a wall-mounted Type 2 7kW charger, although you could install a Type 1 3.5kW charger instead.

Almost all vehicles can use these chargers, but there are obvious problems:

The scheme does not allow you to install chargers which are compatible with a 3-pin plug. This means that the "granny cable" in the boot of your car will be of no use.

The grant is modest, so encourages the installation of wall-mounted units, rather than standalone post-mounted units. This limits each station to only one or two possible car parking stations, whereas a well-positioned post charger could be utilised by four parking spaces.

Given the number of people working from home at moment, it is worth noting that the government is also providing funding towards the cost of installing an electric charging point at a residential property through the Electric Vehicle Homecharge Scheme (EVHS). Similar to the Workplace Charging Scheme, the EVHS provides funding for 75% of the cost of installing one charge point, up to a maximum of £350. If your residence has two EVs, you can apply for two EVHS grants.

The other obvious drawback when these schemes were launched was that the grant did not apply to fast charging stations, just to the slow 7kW chargers we talked about earlier. The Government presumably considered that 7kW allows fast charging, but it will still take 4 hours to charge a standard battery. In other words, each charging station would be occupied for half a day – in reality, how would the landlord ensure that cars just received a 1hour top up before having to be moved on? In response to public consultation, the grant has now been extended to include 22kW charging stations, which will still take an hour and a half to give a full charge, but are powerful enough to give a decent top-up in about 20 minutes. This is still a long way short of the super-fast chargers, which can give a full re-charge in 20 minutes.

So, the grant now covers decent semi-fast chargers, but the level of grant remains at £350, which is little more than one third of the cost of such equipment.

By stark contract, the Office for Zero Emission Vehicles has funding available for local authorities, which can apply for a grant to cover part of the capital costs of installing charge points for residents who lack off-street parking. While the voucher available for business owners is capped at £350 per charging point, the grant available for local authorities to install charge points for local residents is £6,500 per charge point, and is actually lower than the previous figure of £7,500 (although during the 2020/21 financial year the higher sum of £7,500 per was retained, if the local authority could show financial need).

The Government's position is that the lower funding per charge point allows the budget to be spread more widely, for the good of the public generally. Politics comes into play here, with the current Government's expressed wish to level the playing field between the South and North of England.

Existing petrol stations: If your clients already operate a fuel filling station, or a motorway service station, then the Government is entitled to require that they provide EV charging points for public use. This is set out in s11 of the Automated and Electric Vehicles Act 2018.

To push this point home, the 2020 Budget launched the Rapid Charging Fund. If the political ambition of ending the use of the internal combustion engine in 2035 is to be realised, then extensive public charging infrastructure across the nation's motorway and major A road network will be essential, regardless of how many homes and offices have charging points.

With figures changing rapidly, at the time of writing any EV being driven on one of England's motorways or major A roads is never more than 25 miles away from a 50 kW rapid charger – on 1st January 2020, there were 809 open-access rapid charge points across the country.

The Rapid Charging Fund brought £500 million to help with EV charging infrastructure, acknowledging that the infrastructure must be ahead of EV ownership, as it is the fear of running out of battery charge that is the key reason for consumers declining to purchase an electric car. This is known as "range anxiety".

The Rapid Charging Fund currently is a little light on detail, but it is intended to provide partial funding for strategically important road locations and will focus on sites where there is a need for charging stations but where installation is not commercially viable. This would suggest that the money will be spent in more remote A road locations, rather than on the core motorway network. Business owners should take note that grant funding will be available for charge points that are up to one mile away from a main road, which hugely increases the number of potential sites, and gives opportunities to landowners outside the highly competitive "junction" areas.

The purpose of the fund is to get rapid chargers into the public domain, in order to drive the popularity of EVs, rather than to install many more of the cheaper slow chargers. It is the Government's ambition that there should be 2,500 fast chargers across England's motorways and major A roads by 2030, with that figure rising to 6,000 by 2035.

Given that the Rapid Charging Fund is paid for by the taxpayer, all charge points installed with the benefit of this money must be available to the public, and suitable for all types of EV. Currently, this means that they will have to have both Type 1 and Type 2 sockets. It follows that grant funding is not available for the latest Tesla Superchargers, as this equipment can only work with Tesla cars, whether or not the Tesla vehicle uses the CCS system or Tesla's own proprietary socket – a Tesla charging station will still only function if the car plugged into it is a Tesla.

As mentioned above, the Government has the power under the Automated and Electric Vehicles Act 2018 to force operators' hands, if they do not press on with installing fast charging points. Grants are available, as are penalties!

Subsidies

Contracts for Difference?

The Government supports new low carbon electricity generators with the Contracts for Difference (CfD) scheme, although this does not apply in Northern Ireland. On-shore wind farms are not currently supported by CfDs.

The main support scheme for new renewable generating stations is through the CfD mechanism which was introduced under the Energy Act 2013. The other schemes such as the Renewables Obligation scheme and the feed-in tariff scheme for certain renewable generators with a maximum capacity of 5MW closed to new capacity in March 2017 and April 2019 respectively.

In May 2019, the UK government announced that it would allow subsidy-free renewable technologies to participate in the UK's capacity market for the first time, and a year later, introduced a carbon emissions threshold and mandatory reporting and verification requirements for participants in the scheme.

Small-scale generation is supported through a smart export guarantee regime, which came into force on 1 January 2020, and requires electricity suppliers of a certain size to offer to enter into contracts with owners of small, low-carbon electricity generation installations. This provides a guaranteed route to market for small-scale renewable generation in the absence of the feed-in tariff regime, although the level of tariff is at the discretion of the individual supplier and the tariffs being offered by some electricity suppliers are as little as 0.5–1.5p / kWh.

Larger generators can apply for a CfD, which is a contract between a generator of low carbon electricity and a Government-owned body called the Low Carbon Contracts Company (LCCC). The generator is paid the difference between the passing average market price for electricity (the "reference price") and the "strike price", which is calculated from a Government schedule which is intended to reflect the cost of investing in each of a list of low carbon technologies. The purpose of CfDs is to provide a stable income stream to investors, who may be put off by the volatility of wholesale electricity prices, while not paying out too much taxpayers' money when wholesale prices are high.

So far, the scheme appears to have succeeded in driving a large increase in capacity while also pushing down costs. Each CfD also requires the generator to improve the technology. The load factor (discussed above) for offshore wind must reach nearly 60% in the next 5 years, while anaerobic digesters are expected to hit 90%.

CfDs currently support 16GW of renewable electricity schemes and are granted in "allocation rounds". The third allocation round took place in September 2019, when the reference prices were well below the strike price for each technology. For example: Offshore wind has a strike price of £56 while large anaerobic digesters have a strike price of £113, but in each case the reference price fluctuates around £50.

The cost of offshore wind fell by around 30% from the 2017 allocation round. Electricity from renewable sources has become cheaper than electricity from traditional sources.

The Low Carbon Contracts Company website keeps a map of all the sites which have been granted a CfD. They are all large generation schemes and there has been complaint that the CfD process is simply a way of subsidising additional wind power capacity. As part of the third allocation round the Department for Business, Energy & Industrial Strategy (BEIS) announced that "less established technologies" – advanced conversion technology (ACT) could participate, along with dedicated biomass, offshore wind and also "remote island wind projects".

Advanced conversion technologies, which aim to bring a hi-tech and much greener approach to generating heat by burning rubbish, or burning as from an anaerobic digester, were given competitive strike prices, but no biomass or biogas projects were granted a CfD in the third allocation round.

In November 2020, the UK government confirmed that there would be significant changes to the CfD scheme for projects competing in allocation round four, which is due to take place in late 2021. The budget allocation "pots" are being revised. Importantly, the Government has abandoned its opposition to subsidising new onshore wind farms and solar power projects.

On-shore wind will return to the CfD scheme. As for floating windfarms, they are being moved from the "off-shore" pot and into the "advanced conversion technologies". Floating wind farms will get their own strike price, but there is concern that this will just enable the Government to give further support to off-shore wind (which now has three categories – offshore/floating/remote island wind) at the expense of biomass and biogas.

Contracts awarded in 2021 run for 5 years, but it is anticipated that the scheme will be extended until at least 2035.

Tax – the Balfour Assessment

Farm, and many other trading businesses, can be very tax efficient when the owners reach the end of their lives and the business is passed to the next generation.

Business property relief and agricultural property relief are available to mitigate the Impact of Inheritance Tax. However, BPR and APR are only available to trading businesses.

If you turn your farm (a trading business) Into a solar farm (an Income yielding Investment business) then APR and BRP will no longer be available to the relevant parts of the old farming business. The risk to the Inheriting family Is that these reliefs will be lost entirely.

Tax Is far too complicated to discuss in detail here but be aware of the Balfour Assessment.

In short, HM Revenue and Customs will look at the tax affairs of the business and will look in particular at:

- How much turnover and profit do the various parts of the farming business make?
- What are the capital values of those respective parts?
- How much resource/time/staff hours do the various parts of the business require?

When taken as a whole, having considered these questions, Is the farm a trading business or an investment business?

To avoid this assessment falling on the wrong side, the business owners should consider splitting the farm, by hiving the solar farm off into a separate business entity.

This of course requires specialist advice!

MORE BOOKS BY LAW BRIEF PUBLISHING

A selection of our other titles available now:-

'A Practical Guide to the Independent School Standards – September 2023 Edition' by Sarah McKimm
'A Practical Guide to Estate Administration and Crypto Assets' by Richard Marshall
'A Practical Guide to Managing GDPR Data Subject Access Requests – Second Edition' by Patrick O'Kane
'A Practical Guide to Parental Alienation in Private and Public Law Children Cases' by Sam King QC & Frankie Shama
'Contested Heritage – Removing Art from Land and Historic Buildings' by Richard Harwood QC, Catherine Dobson, David Sawtell
'The Limits of Separate Legal Personality: When Those Running a Company Can Be Held Personally Liable for Losses Caused to Third Parties Outside of the Company' by Dr Mike Wilkinson
'A Practical Guide to Transgender Law' by Robin Moira White & Nicola Newbegin
'A Practical Guide to 'Stranded Spouses' in Family Law' by Mani Singh Basi
'A Practical Guide to Residential Freehold Conveyancing' by Lorraine Richardson
'A Practical Guide to Pensions on Divorce for Lawyers' by Bryan Scant
'A Practical Guide to Challenging Sham Marriage Allegations in Immigration Law' by Priya Solanki
'A Practical Guide to Digital Communications Evidence in Criminal Law' by Sam Willis
'A Practical Guide to Legal Rights in Scotland' by Sarah-Jane Macdonald
'A Practical Guide to New Build Conveyancing' by Paul Sams & Rebecca East
'A Practical Guide to Defending Barristers in Disciplinary Cases' by Marc Beaumont
'A Practical Guide to Inherited Wealth on Divorce' by Hayley Trim
'A Practical Guide to Practice Direction 12J and Domestic Abuse in Private Law Children Proceedings' by Rebecca Cross & Malvika Jaganmohan

'A Practical Guide to Confiscation and Restraint' by Narita Bahra QC, John Carl Townsend, David Winch
'A Practical Guide to the Law of Forests in Scotland' by Philip Buchan
'A Practical Guide to Health and Medical Cases in Immigration Law' by Rebecca Chapman & Miranda Butler
'A Practical Guide to Bad Character Evidence for Criminal Practitioners by Aparna Rao
'A Practical Guide to Extradition Law post-Brexit' by Myles Grandison et al
'A Practical Guide to Hoarding and Mental Health for Housing Lawyers' by Rachel Coyle
'A Practical Guide to Psychiatric Claims in Personal Injury – 2nd Edition' by Liam Ryan
'Stephens on Contractual Indemnities' by Richard Stephens
'A Practical Guide to the EU Succession Regulation' by Richard Frimston
'A Practical Guide to Solicitor and Client Costs – 2nd Edition' by Robin Dunne
'Constructive Dismissal – Practice Pointers and Principles' by Benjimin Burgher
'A Practical Guide to Religion and Belief Discrimination Claims in the Workplace' by Kashif Ali
'A Practical Guide to the Law of Medical Treatment Decisions' by Ben Troke
'Fundamental Dishonesty and QOCS in Personal Injury Proceedings: Law and Practice' by Jake Rowley
'A Practical Guide to the Law in Relation to School Exclusions' by Charlotte Hadfield & Alice de Coverley
'A Practical Guide to Divorce for the Silver Separators' by Karin Walker
'The Right to be Forgotten – The Law and Practical Issues' by Melissa Stock
'A Practical Guide to Planning Law and Rights of Way in National Parks, the Broads and AONBs' by James Maurici QC, James Neill et al
'A Practical Guide to Election Law' by Tom Tabori
'A Practical Guide to the Law in Relation to Surrogacy' by Andrew Powell
'A Practical Guide to Claims Arising from Fatal Accidents – 2nd Edition' by James Patience
'A Practical Guide to the Ownership of Employee Inventions – From Entitlement to Compensation' by James Tumbridge & Ashley Roughton
'A Practical Guide to Asbestos Claims' by Jonathan Owen & Gareth McAloon

'A Practical Guide to Stamp Duty Land Tax in England and Northern Ireland' by Suzanne O'Hara

'A Practical Guide to the Law of Farming Partnerships' by Philip Whitcomb

'Covid-19, Homeworking and the Law – The Essential Guide to Employment and GDPR Issues' by Forbes Solicitors

'Covid-19 and Criminal Law – The Essential Guide' by Ramya Nagesh

'Covid-19 and Family Law in England and Wales – The Essential Guide' by Safda Mahmood

'A Practical Guide to the Law of Unlawful Eviction and Harassment – 2nd Edition' by Stephanie Lovegrove

'Covid-19, Brexit and the Law of Commercial Leases – The Essential Guide' by Mark Shelton

'A Practical Guide to Costs in Personal Injury Claims – 2nd Edition' by Matthew Hoe

'A Practical Guide to the General Data Protection Regulation (GDPR) – 2nd Edition' by Keith Markham

'Ellis on Credit Hire – Sixth Edition' by Aidan Ellis & Tim Kevan

'A Practical Guide to Working with Litigants in Person and McKenzie Friends in Family Cases' by Stuart Barlow

'Protecting Unregistered Brands: A Practical Guide to the Law of Passing Off' by Lorna Brazell

'A Practical Guide to Secondary Liability and Joint Enterprise Post-Jogee' by Joanne Cecil & James Mehigan

'A Practical Guide to the Pre-Action RTA Claims Protocol for Personal Injury Lawyers' by Antonia Ford

'A Practical Guide to Neighbour Disputes and the Law' by Alexander Walsh

'A Practical Guide to Forfeiture of Leases' by Mark Shelton

'A Practical Guide to Coercive Control for Legal Practitioners and Victims' by Rachel Horman

'A Practical Guide to the Law of Driverless Cars – Second Edition' by Alex Glassbrook, Emma Northey & Scarlett Milligan

'A Practical Guide to TOLATA Claims' by Greg Williams

'A Practical Guide to Elderly Law – 2nd Edition' by Justin Patten

'A Practical Guide to Responding to Housing Disrepair and Unfitness Claims' by Iain Wightwick

‘A Practical Guide to the Law of Bullying and Harassment in the Workplace’ by Philip Hyland

‘How to Be a Freelance Solicitor: A Practical Guide to the SRA-Regulated Freelance Solicitor Model’ by Paul Bennett

‘A Practical Guide to Prison Injury Claims’ by Malcolm Johnson

‘A Practical Guide to the Small Claims Track – 2nd Edition’ by Dominic Bright

‘A Practical Guide to Advising Clients at the Police Station’ by Colin Stephen McKeown-Beaumont

‘A Practical Guide to Antisocial Behaviour Injunctions’ by Iain Wightwick

‘Practical Mediation: A Guide for Mediators, Advocates, Advisers, Lawyers, and Students in Civil, Commercial, Business, Property, Workplace, and Employment Cases’ by Jonathan Dingle with John Sephton

‘The Mini-Pupillage Workbook’ by David Boyle

‘A Practical Guide to Crofting Law’ by Brian Inkster

‘A Practical Guide to the Law of Domain Names and Cybersquatting’ by Andrew Clemson

‘A Practical Guide to the Law of Gender Pay Gap Reporting’ by Harini Iyengar

‘NHS Whistleblowing and the Law’ by Joseph England

‘Employment Law and the Gig Economy’ by Nigel Mackay & Annie Powell

‘A Practical Guide to Noise Induced Hearing Loss (NIHL) Claims’ by Andrew Mckie, Ian Skeate, Gareth McAloon

‘An Introduction to Beauty Negligence Claims – A Practical Guide for the Personal Injury Practitioner’ by Greg Almond

‘Intercompany Agreements for Transfer Pricing Compliance’ by Paul Sutton

‘Zen and the Art of Mediation’ by Martin Plowman

‘A Practical Guide to the SRA Principles, Individual and Law Firm Codes of Conduct 2019 – What Every Law Firm Needs to Know’ by Paul Bennett

‘A Practical Guide to Adoption for Family Lawyers’ by Graham Pegg

‘A Practical Guide to Industrial Disease Claims’ by Andrew Mckie & Ian Skeate

‘A Practical Guide to Conducting a Sheriff Court Proof’ by Andrew Stevenson

‘A Practical Guide to Vicarious Liability’ by Mariel Irvine

‘A Practical Guide to Applications for Landlord’s Consent and Variation of Leases’ by Mark Shelton

‘A Practical Guide to Relief from Sanctions Post-Mitchell and Denton’ by Peter Causton

'A Practical Guide to Equity Release for Advisors' by Paul Sams
'A Practical Guide to Financial Services Claims' by Chris Hegarty
'The Law of Houses in Multiple Occupation: A Practical Guide to HMO Proceedings' by Julian Hunt
'Occupiers, Highways and Defective Premises Claims: A Practical Guide Post-Jackson – 2nd Edition' by Andrew Mckie
'A Practical Guide to Financial Ombudsman Service Claims' by Adam Temple & Robert Scrivenor
'A Practical Guide to Running Housing Disrepair and Cavity Wall Claims: 2nd Edition' by Andrew Mckie & Ian Skeate
'A Practical Guide to Holiday Sickness Claims – 2nd Edition' by Andrew Mckie & Ian Skeate
'Arguments and Tactics for Personal Injury and Clinical Negligence Claims' by Dorian Williams
'A Practical Guide to Drone Law' by Rufus Ballaster, Andrew Firman, Eleanor Clot
'A Practical Guide to Compliance for Personal Injury Firms Working With Claims Management Companies' by Paul Bennett
'RTA Allegations of Fraud in a Post-Jackson Era: The Handbook – 2nd Edition' by Andrew Mckie
'RTA Personal Injury Claims: A Practical Guide Post-Jackson' by Andrew Mckie
'On Experts: CPR35 for Lawyers and Experts' by David Boyle
'An Introduction to Personal Injury Law' by David Boyle

www.ingramcontent.com/pod-product-compliance
Lightning Source LLC
LaVergne TN
LVHW022100200926
848481LV00003B/1008
9781916698376